MW00605429

TENDING *the* WOUND *of* SEXUAL ABUSE

TENDING *the* WOUND *of* SEXUAL ABUSE

An Introduction

ANTHONY DELMEDICO, PHD

FIRST HAVEN
RALEIGH, NORTH CAROLINA

Published by First Haven
901 Paverstone Drive, Suite 9
Raleigh, North Carolina 27615
www.FirstHaven.org

Copyright © 2022 First Haven

All rights reserved. No part of this book may be reprinted or reproduced or utilized in any form or by any electronic, mechanical, or other means, now known or hereafter invented, including photocopying and recording, or in any information storage or retrieval system, without permission in writing from the publishers, except by a reviewer who may quote passages in a review.

Library of Congress Cataloguing in Publication Data

Name: Delmedico, Anthony, author.
Title: Tending the Wound of Sexual Abuse: An Introduction
Description: Raleigh, North Carolina: First Haven [2022] | Includes
    bibliographical references.
Identifiers: LCCN 2022900572 (print) | ISBN 978-1-7346308-3-1 (pbk.:
    alk. paper)
Subjects: Self-help | Mental Health Counseling | Psychology | Sexual Abuse
    Victims | Trauma

Cover design by Patricia Delmedico and Hilary Stoddard
Cover image by Chelsea Hopkins-Allen. *Balancing Stones No. 1*, watercolor on cotton
    rag paper, 2013. Used with permission.

Set in Adobe Caslon Pro with P22 Underground Pro Book
Printed in the United States of America

Neither the publisher nor the author is engaged in rendering professional advice or services to the individual reader. The ideas, procedures, and suggestions in this book are not intended as a substitute for consulting with your physician, psychiatrist, and trauma-informed mental health practitioner. All matters regarding your physical and mental health require supervision by the proper professionals. Neither the author nor the publisher shall be liable or responsible for any loss or damage allegedly arising from any information or suggestion in this book.

"In a dark time, the eye begins to see."

Theodore Roethke

CONTENTS

IV
GETTING CALM AND STABLE

V
GOING DEEPER

VI
THE WAY AHEAD

PREFACE

The wound of sexual abuse is unlike any other. As you may now know, it can cut all the way to your core. Even though you might be feeling quite alone right now, you are not. Unfortunately, sexual abuse, in some form or another, occurs everywhere in the world, and it has throughout history. It can and does happen to anyone, at any age, regardless of gender, race, or sexual identity. Even with sexual abuse being so widespread, your experience is uniquely yours. This guide was written to help you understand this deep wound—your wound—as best you can in order to learn how to tend it properly. It also introduces you to some essential skills, tools, and techniques that are very helpful when dealing with this wound.

In addition to my own personal and professional experience, inspiration for this guide also came from reading Dr. Laura Kerr's year-long blog *Ambivalent Goddesses: Recovering from Sexual Trauma.* Her *Live Within Your Window of Tolerance* guide may still be available for download.[1] Additionally, I wish to acknowledge the significant contributions made to this guide by J. Doe I and J. Doe II, two people who were sexually abused by a person in a position of power. I refer to them by the names assigned to them by the legal system to protect their confidentiality since they were both minors when their abuse occurred. Their perspectives, insights, editing efforts, and design ideas for this guide have been invaluable.

I have a doctoral degree in depth psychology with an emphasis in depth psychotherapy. I am trauma trained psychotherapist who has worked with children and adults of all ages who have experienced sexual abuse. This guide is grounded in evidence-based treatment standards and leading theories about what can happen psychologically when someone experiences sexual abuse. It introduces some best practices to help you understand and tend the wound of sexual abuse.

Finally, if you have received this guide at no cost, it is because someone believes in you and your ability to heal and has made a contribution to First Haven, a 501(c)(3) nonprofit organization, which produces this guide. All donations and any profit from the sale of this guide are used to print and distribute more copies at no charge to agencies and institutions that specialize in working with people who have experienced sexual abuse. Go to FirstHaven.org to make a donation, leave a comment, or purchase additional copies. With your donation, you can also specify where you would like copies sent. See the Donate page at the end of the guide for more information.

INTRODUCTION

This guide is intended for people ages 15 and up who have experienced sexual abuse. If you care for someone who has been sexually abused, reading this guide will also provide insight and greater understanding.[1] The model for sexual abuse recovery used in the guide is proven and time tested. While grounded in 150 years of trauma research and depth psychology,[2] it is also based upon current evidence-based best practices for working through the trauma of sexual abuse.[3] The model is founded on our natural instinct to protect ourselves and heal when we get wounded and on our innate desire to feel OK again.

This guide is not intended as a band-aid. Instead, it speaks directly to some of the most difficult things one can encounter in the aftermath of sexual abuse. Reading the guide and doing the exercises will also reduce the chances of this kind of trauma being repeated in your life. Moreover, it will help you begin to heal and feel better. It will also help make it easier to move forward with your life and become the person you choose to be.

Because this guide is an introduction, it is limited in scope. You may find that some key issues and major themes pertaining to your experience of sexual abuse have been wholly overlooked or omitted. As you become aware of the guide's limitations and deficits, seek out the additional information and support needed as you care for yourself and do the work of deep healing.

Organization

The guide has six parts. Part I defines sexual abuse and describes its potential impact. Part II prepares you for working with this special kind of wound and helps lay a strong foundation for success. Part III increases your awareness of how sexual abuse may be affecting you now and provides ways to think about and organize your experiences. In Part IV, you will learn how to calm your mind and body so that you can tolerate uncomfortable memories and sensations more easily. Part V invites you to go deeper and teaches you how to deal with strong emotions, inner critics, and numbness so that you can work through and resolve them. You will also learn how to work with nightmares, identify traumatic memories, and address flashbacks if you are having them. Finally, Part VI prepares you for what to expect in the months and years ahead.

Throughout the guide, you are reminded that authentic healing takes time and does not happen in a straight line. It is not as simple as 1-2-3. (If only it were so easy!) The healing of deep wounds is *circular* in nature. Things get worked and reworked as you go through different stages in life. You are unique and complex, and sexual abuse affects each person differently. So, be patient and gentle with yourself as you work through this guide and get things figured out.

Style and Terminology

For ease of reading, in-text citations have been minimized. Endnotes and bibliography are found at the end of the guide.

Affirming diversity, gender-neutral and gender-inclusive pronouns are used throughout this guide.

People use different words to think and talk about their sexual abuse. You might describe your experience using words and phrases like "rape," "being molested," "dating," "a weird relationship," or "just something that happened." I have chosen to use the terms "sexual abuse" and "the experience of sexual abuse" throughout this guide. See if you can stay with the material even if these phrases don't exactly fit for you.

The terms "victim" and "survivor" are commonly used to describe those who have experienced sexual abuse. While you have certainly been a victim of sexual abuse and are a survivor, those terms are not used in the guide because, when used as labels, they have the potential to become self-limiting or reductionistic. Regardless of the wound, a fundamental task in each person's life is to become the hero or heroine in their own story.[4] Being sexually abused is an experience that cannot be forgotten, and it is now a part of your story. It informs the heroic journey leading you to the deepest parts of yourself.

The terms "wound" and "the wound of sexual abuse" are used throughout the guide. It can be helpful to know you are not a "wounded person." Rather, you are a person who has suffered a special kind of wound that requires a special kind of care. This guide is an introduction on how to do just that.

A decision was also made not to include accounts of others who have been sexually abused because there can be a tendency for the mind to use them for comparison. Every situation is different, and each person is unique. What matters most is what happened to you and how it may be affecting you—specifically. To that end, the guide provides you with a framework to work through your own experience.

How to Use this Guide

It can be hard to read at a time like this because you may be wanting to avoid painful thoughts and memories, so work through this guide at your own pace. Most chapters are short and can be read in just a few minutes. When you are reading, try to actively work with the material. Highlight things that resonate. Make comments in the margins. At the end of each chapter, there is a "What's true for you?" section prompting you to dig deeper about what goes on inside of you. Do these exercises! They will help you learn how to tend the wound of your sexual abuse.

Finally, hold on to this guide. If it is too difficult to read right now, put it aside and come back to it later when you are ready. You can also return to it at various times in life whenever your wound needs some extra attention.

Disclaimer

This guide is NOT a substitute for getting help and working with a trauma-trained therapist (and psychiatrist, if needed). Use this guide as a supplement to the other support you are getting. If you are not working with someone already, do an internet search if you have access, or ask your doctor for a referral. See Appendix A for a list of online resources.

I

ABOUT SEXUAL ABUSE

1

SEXUAL ABUSE AND TREATMENT

S EXUAL abuse can cause you to become unsure of yourself. It may cause you even to have doubts about what happened. This chapter defines sexual abuse in order to help you get clarity about your situation. It also introduces some of the ways in which sexual abuse can affect you if left untreated. Finally, it provides information about the types of treatment available to aid in your healing efforts.

As you read the following definitions of sexual abuse, determine which aspects apply for you. If self-doubts return, come back to these definitions to help remain clear about what happened.

Sexual Abuse Defined

The American Psychological Association defines sexual abuse as any unwanted sexual activity where perpetrators use force, make threats, or take advantage of victims who are not able to give consent.[1] The Unites States Department of Justice (DOJ) defines sexual assault as any nonconsensual sexual act against Federal, State, or Tribal law. It also includes situations where the victim lacks the capacity to give consent.[2] The DOJ defines rape as "the penetration, no matter how slight, of the vagina or anus with any body part or object, or oral penetration by a sex organ of another person, without the consent of the victim."[3]

Regarding minors (typically someone under the age of 18), the World Health Organization defines sexual abuse as the involvement of a minor in any sexual activity that they don't fully understand, is unable to give *informed consent* to, are not developmentally ready for, or that violate the laws or social taboos of society. This includes any sexual activity between a minor and an adult (or another minor) who, by age or development, is in a relationship of responsibility, trust, or power.[4]

Sexual abuse of minors includes a range of activities that can involve force or no force, as well as contact or no contact at all.[5] This includes fondling directly or over clothing, attempted intercourse, intercourse, oral-genital contact, exhibitionism, using minors for pornography or prostitution, or exposing them to adult sexual activity or pornography.[6]

Finally, in the eyes of the law, you must be considered to be of "legal age of majority" to give informed consent. Therefore, all sexual activity between an adult and an underage minor (even with the minor's permission) is, by definition, child sexual abuse.[7]

Potential Impact of Sexual Abuse

Studies have shown that sexual abuse can affect how a person thinks, acts, and feels over a lifetime. People who have been sexually abused are at higher risk for developing posttraumatic stress disorder (PTSD), anxiety, depression, an eating disorder, a sleep disorder, and have an increased risk of suicide attempts.[8] They can also carry higher levels of anger, guilt, and shame. There is also a higher risk of developing drug or alcohol problems and an increased risk of being revictimized. Later in life, there is an increased risk of having relational, sexual, or family issues.[9] Additionally, physical health can be impacted over time as a result of sexual abuse.[10]

The potential aftereffects in the previous paragraph are quite serious. However, sexual abuse has historically been underreported and, as a result, gone largely untreated.[11] Without treatment, the things mentioned above can be seen as some of the ways in which the mind and body try to deal with sexual abuse. This information is provided so that you know what to be watchful for in your own life. Learning how to tend the wound of sexual abuse and getting proper treatment lower your risk of developing issues like those listed above.[12] Rather than trying to avoid what happened, you owe it to yourself to begin dealing with it now. This guide will help show you how.

Treatment for Sexual Abuse

As you read and work through this guide, you will be educating yourself about the wound of sexual abuse and learning how to tend it, but getting proper treatment when needed is also essential. You will benefit greatly from working with a trauma-trained therapist in your efforts to heal.

Many different kinds of trauma-trained mental health professionals practice in diverse settings using various approaches to work with those who have experienced sexual abuse. These include psychoanalysts, psychotherapists, clinical psychologists, mental health counselors, social workers, marriage and family therapists, play therapists, and art therapists, to name a few.

Treatment can occur in individual, family, or group settings. Before beginning, ask the therapist how they work and make sure this aligns with your preferences. Also, ask about their confidentiality policy as it may vary depending upon the setting and your age.

Sexual abuse can be treated using a variety of approaches, including talk therapy, body-centered therapy, play therapy, art therapy, or some combination thereof. Currently, some of the more widely used techniques include Eye Movement Desensitization and Reprocessing (EMDR),[13] trauma-focused cognitive behavior therapies (TF-CBT),[14] trauma-informed talk therapy,[15] and cognitive processing therapy.[16] There are also other treatments being used, and new therapies continue to emerge and evolve.

Selecting a Therapist

While this guide does not endorse a particular type of therapist or treatment modality, choosing a licensed therapist with trauma training is important. When you meet with them for the first time, ask about their training and approach to working with sexual abuse. Finally, it is also strongly recommended that you work with someone who makes you feel comfortable, safe, and inspires confidence.[17] If you do not have any recommendations for a therapist or are not working with someone already, do an internet search for therapists in your area specializing in the treatment of sexual abuse. If you are unsure or uncomfortable after your first meeting, meet with another therapist (or two) until you find a good fit for yourself.

What's true for you?

What scared you the most when you read the "Potential Impact of Sexual Abuse" section in this chapter? You will need to be on the lookout for those things in the coming months and years.

What practical steps can you take now to begin working with a trauma-trained therapist?

2

A Special Kind of Wound

WHEN someone is abused sexually, a special kind of wound is created that requires a special kind of care. It will not go away if you try to ignore it.[1] This is the kind of wound that requires *tending*. But you may argue that all wounds close up and heal and that "whatever doesn't kill you makes you stronger." That may be true for a broken bone or a cut, but the deep wounds of the mind and the heart are different. These injuries are so big that they can be considered life wounds or *soul wounds* because they affect us so profoundly.[2] Sooner or later, almost everybody gets at least one big soul wound in life.

Sexual abuse is the type of wound that requires being looked after, much like a plant that every so often needs water, sunlight, and some tender loving care. If you are suffering inside, it may help to know that there is nothing wrong with you even if it has been a while—weeks, months, even years—since your abuse occurred. Even just the scab for this kind of wound can take a long time to form. Things can stay raw for quite some time.

People have all kinds of different reactions after being sexually abused. For example, some try to hide it or ignore it. Some even try to convince themselves that it didn't really happen. Others disconnect and numb out in an attempt to protect themselves from unwanted memories or feelings. These types of reactions are common because they often serve to protect one's self, the one(s) who did it, friends, or family members.[3] Alternately, some people begin acting out in dangerous ways. Take an honest look at yourself. How do you think that you have reacted after your sexual abuse?

Many who have experienced sexual abuse try to bury it as deeply as possible in the hope that it will just go away. Many keep it secret for decades.[4] Some never tell anyone and suffer in silence their whole lives. Studies have shown that remaining silent causes its own psychological problems and can lead to mental health issues as well.[5] So, trying to bury your abuse can end up causing more pain for you in the long run. Since the mind and body do not forget,[6] it is best to learn about this special kind of wound in order to better care for it—and yourself. Reading this guide, doing the exercises, and getting the support you need will help you learn how to do this.[7]

Being sexually abused is also a violation in the deepest sense and brings with it a profound loss of innocence both sexually and psychologically.[8] This is true even if you were sexually curious or active before. Because of your sexual abuse, you have learned some difficult truths all too soon. You may have also had some of your core beliefs shaken to their foundations as well. You now know that life is not fair, that the world can be a dangerous place, and that some people cannot be trusted. You also now know that really bad things can happen to anyone.

What happened to you was not fair. You did not deserve this wound, and no one should ever have to go through what you went through. But it did happen to you. And sadly, it remains a widespread and ongoing reality.[9] See Appendix B for a list of famous people who were sexually abused. While it is good to know that you are not alone on your journey, you also need to know that you will have to do the work yourself. No one else can do it for you.

Learning to tend the wound of sexual abuse is challenging because there is no one else in the world who is just like you. There is no "one size fits all" when it comes to healing. Each person is affected differently and goes through it in their own way. While this guide lays out the territory you are likely to encounter, the journey is uniquely yours.

What's true for you?

Since you now know sexual abuse is a special kind of wound that requires special care, how does this change your thinking about it and yourself?

Sexual abuse has been described as a profound violation and a loss of innocence. What do you feel like you have lost as a result of your experience of sexual abuse? What might need to be reclaimed? What do you now know that you didn't before?

3

DIFFICULT MEMORIES

W OULDN'T it be nice to erase all the horrible things that happen to us in life? Unfortunately, we do not have a delete button; the mind does not work like that. Instead, whether we like it or not, each of us is a storehouse of memories. Our minds and our bodies store all of our experiences in life, whether we can consciously remember them or not.[1]

Because our memories cannot be erased, we only have a couple of options for dealing with them. When unwanted memories or bodily sensations arise, we can either (a) ignore them or push them away or (b) work with them. Unfortunately, if you try to push them away, they only gain power and just keep coming back.[2] And if you keep ignoring them, they will start negatively affecting you in other ways. Since you will have to deal with them sooner or later, why not learn how to do it now? It will save you a lot of misery in the long run.

It is not easy to ask yourself to go toward the very things you may have been trying to avoid. Sometimes, it may require great psychological courage. If you have some fear or reluctance, work with a trauma-trained therapist. They specialize in this kind of work and can provide proper treatment and support in dealing with difficult and disturbing memories. Over and over again, this guide will invite you to slow your mind down, pay closer attention to what is happening inside you, turn toward the difficult things, and learn how to work *with* them. With practice, you should be able to use those skills *most* of the time. Once you can do that, you will be well on your way to becoming an expert on tending the wound of your sexual abuse.

Notice the phrase "*most* of the time" in the previous paragraph. You should know that these things are impossible for anyone to do *all* the time. For whatever reason, sometimes the memories or sensations are just too overwhelming. It doesn't mean you have failed or that all of your work was in vain when that happens. It just means that it was tough to deal with—that time! You are only human, and this is really hard stuff. Learning how to tolerate difficult memories and sensations while still taking good care of yourself when you get overwhelmed takes time and practice. (The people around you may not even know how to do it.) Reading and working through this guide will give you the skills, practice, and confidence you need.

What's true for you?
Working through your experience of sexual abuse is difficult to do and takes courage. What fears do you have about learning how to go toward and work with difficult memories or uncomfortable bodily sensations?

4

MAKING SENSE

WHEN thinking about your experience of sexual abuse, it is normal to feel some confusion around what happened and where to place the blame.[1] Because sexual abuse is so hard to make sense of, people sometimes try to blame themselves for what happened.[2] This is a common thing for the mind to do because it provides you with some feeling of control in a situation that was out of control.[3] But blaming yourself doesn't help, and making yourself the scapegoat doesn't heal. (And it is simply not true!) Also, other people's reactions to your sexual abuse can vary widely and be very different from your own, which may cause further confusion. This chapter explores why it can be hard to make sense of sexual abuse and provides tips on how to talk with others as you sort through it.

Below are four reasons why it is hard to make sense of sexual abuse. As you read them, think about which ones apply in your situation.

Self-blame

While trying to make sense of your sexual abuse, you may try to blame yourself instead of the person or people who did this to you. The following are examples of self-blaming statements:

- I took the wrong way home.
- I wore the wrong thing.
- I was careless.
- I deserved it.
- I drank too much or got too high.
- I trusted someone that I had every right to trust.
- I am being punished because I am bad.
- I should have known better.
- I was warned.
- I didn't fight back or fight it enough.
- I didn't say no.
- I participated.
- My body was aroused.
- I came on to them.
- I felt loved, special, unique, or powerful.

Have you found yourself using any of these statements in an effort to blame yourself for what happened? If left unchecked, self-blame can be dangerous. It can affect how you feel about yourself, change your ideas about who you are, and even affect your educational and career choices. It can also change your views about the life and love you deserve.[4] Catch yourself whenever your mind starts down the path of self-blame. Slow your thinking down. Step-by-step, walk yourself back to, "Hey, wait a minute. Being sexually abused actually *wasn't* my fault. I didn't deserve to have this happen to me." Even just a teaspoon a day of these accurate thoughts about yourself can be very beneficial.[5]

13

Confusing and Overwhelming Emotions and Bodily Sensations

Depending on the circumstances and who violated you, you may have felt fear, shame, rage, nausea, helplessness, and betrayal. You may have also felt sexually or emotionally aroused, which can be very confusing and wrongly contribute to self-blame. On the other hand, you may have felt numb or nothing at all. Or, you may have experienced all of these things together at once. It can be hard to make sense of such complex and complicated feelings and sensations.

Your Own Beliefs

In trying to make sense of sexual abuse, you may question your own beliefs about yourself.[6] It can make you feel like you are permanently damaged, unclean, evil, bad, or worthless. It can also make you feel like an imposter now. These things are not true, but those types of feelings can be strong, and those thoughts have power. If you are not careful, you can end up spending a lot of time beating yourself up for what happened.[7] So, be on the lookout for what your beliefs and inner criticisms are doing to you. Once you recognize these self-destructive thoughts, interrupt them if you can, and replace them with the truth. For example, instead of "I'm bad," you can more correctly say, "I'm *not* bad, but a really bad thing did happen to me."

If you are a person of faith, you may also be struggling with your religious beliefs. After the experience of sexual abuse, people can often find themselves having a crisis of faith.[8] Many feel abandoned or forsaken and question their relationship with God or their place of worship.

The World Around You

Finally, making sense of sexual abuse is also challenging because many family members, friends, communities, organizations, schools, and religious institutions still blame, shame, or punish those who have been sexually abused.[9] As a result, you may feel attacked, left out, isolated, or scapegoated.

Even though times are changing in some parts of the world, many who have experienced sexual abuse are still unfairly blamed, either partially or wholly. Many are still pressured to remain silent and are ostracized. This can make you feel abandoned or punished when you are not at fault.

Tips for Talking with Others

Talking with others about your experience of sexual abuse can often provide clarity and be beneficial in your efforts to make sense of it all. Also, sometimes it just feels good to sit and talk about it with someone you trust. However, you may find that many people don't know what to do when you share your thoughts, feelings, and emotions connected to your sexual abuse. They may want to jump in and try to help you, or they may do the opposite and shut down. Some might even get angry at you. Everyone handles things differently. Since most people don't know what to do, give them some guidance.

When you get ready to share with someone, help prepare them. Tell them how you want them to listen. Give directions. Be specific. Here is an example of how to ask a trusted friend or loved one to listen:

"I want to talk with you about some hard stuff, but I'm afraid that it might be too much for you. But I trust you, and I feel like talking about it. Is that OK?

"I just need for you to listen. You don't have to do anything other than that. I'm not looking for advice, and I don't want to be told what to do. I don't need you to fix anything. I just want you to listen and be supportive. You can ask me questions if you get curious about something."

As you talk with them, you might have to remind them again that you are not looking for advice and that they can just relax and listen. When you are done, be sure to thank them! It is a big thing to hold space for someone in this way. Friends and family members may not be able to listen in this manner, but a therapist *is* trained to listen deeply and can support you at every juncture.

What's true for you?

Do you blame yourself in some way for your sexual abuse? If so, how? What can you tell yourself instead that is more accurate?

If you do not have someone already, what steps can you take to find someone to talk to about your sexual abuse?

II

SAFETY PRECAUTIONS

5

KEEP TRYING

THIS section of the guide provides important safety information, prepares you to work with the wound of sexual abuse, and helps lay a strong foundation for success. It will help you identify the supports you may need along the way, and it will teach you how to get the different parts of your mind working together in your efforts to heal. In preparation for the work ahead, this chapter helps you get clear upfront about your reasons for wanting to do this work in the first place.

Tending this wound is challenging. This guide invites you to do some hard work to get to know yourself as best you can in order to tend the wound of your sexual abuse. Many people who have experienced sexual abuse say that they try hard for a while, and then, all of a sudden, they just feel like giving up. If you have had this experience, it is especially important for you to remember why you want to keep trying when things feel bleak.

Think about why you want to keep trying—*especially* when you are in times of despair. For example, maybe you are tired of being consumed by what happened, want to have a healthy relationship, or want to feel good about yourself again. The reasons are different for everybody. Before moving ahead, pause for a moment and decide on your own particular reasons for wanting to do this work. Answer the following question:

Why do you want to keep trying?

It is hard to remember your reasons when you get overwhelmed or feel like giving up. It is also quite a challenge to keep taking good care of yourself during those times. By having your own goals and taking steps toward them, you begin to honor yourself as you learn to tend the wound.

What's true for you?
Have you thought about your reasons for wanting to deal with your sexual abuse? Go to Appendix C, "Why Keep Trying," and make your list now. If it is safe, cut it out and put it where you can see it every day. Add to it over time. Re-read it when you are having difficult times.

6

SUICIDAL THINKING

IN the previous chapter, you were asked to identify your own personal reasons for wanting to work through your sexual abuse. Before getting started with this work, it is important to first educate yourself about a serious issue that can potentially be life-threatening. Studies show that those who experience sexual abuse are at a higher risk of having suicidal thoughts and attempting suicide.[1] This, of course, is frightening for everyone. For most people, suicide is hard to talk about and explore because of the potential consequences. However, like everything else in this guide, you will be invited to go toward the difficult and frightening things in an effort to heal. This chapter is no exception. It will provide you with some very important safety information, and it will teach you how to properly deal with suicidal thoughts if you have them.

If you have thoughts of suicide, you owe it to yourself to stay alive—even if you don't want to sometimes. On some days and in some moments, you may have to fight with everything you have to do it. Turn to Appendix B again and look at the list of famous people who experienced sexual abuse. Remind yourself that you are not alone.

It is also important to become more informed about suicidal thinking so that you know what to do about it. There are two kinds of suicidal thoughts:

- *Passive* suicidal thoughts are thoughts about wishing you were dead but not having a specific plan for how to kill yourself. They include thoughts like, "I wish I were dead," "Everyone would just be better off without me," or "It would be nice if I just got killed in an accident."
- *Active* suicidal thoughts are thoughts where you intend on killing yourself. With active suicidal thinking, you have a plan in place, the means to do it, and a time set for it.

What to Do with Passive Suicidal Thoughts

It is not unusual to have passive suicidal thoughts after experiencing sexual abuse.[2] Let someone you trust know about them. Therapists are trained to work with both active and passive suicidal thoughts. Talk about these thoughts in therapy so that you work through them fully. If you do, you will learn that it is OK to feel really, really bad sometimes and yet *still* go on living.

What to Do with Active Suicidal Thoughts

If you are having active suicidal thoughts, you are in a very dangerous situation. **Get help immediately!** Tell someone right away. If you have a therapist or psychiatrist, call their office and tell them what is happening. If you don't have one, then tell a caregiver, loved one, teacher, coach, school administrator, employer, work colleague, friend, or a friend's parent. In the United States, you can call 911 or go to your nearest emergency room. Call one of the suicide hotline numbers listed below. If you text, use the Crisis Text Line. Someone is available and waiting 24 hours a day, 7 days a week:

National Suicide Hotline: 1-800-273-TALK (8255)

Crisis Text Line: Text 741741

LGBTQ+ Suicide Hotline: 1-866-488-7386

If you are not in the United States, take a moment now and look up the relevant numbers in your country. If you have a cell phone, add those numbers to your contacts even if you are not suicidal. Someday, you may have a friend or loved one that may need support. Remember:

- *Passive* suicidal thoughts: Bring them to therapy and work them through.
- *Active* suicidal thoughts: Let someone know right away! Call a Suicide Hotline or text the Crisis Line.

How Suicidal Thinking Can Trick You

If you have suicidal thoughts, determine whether they are active or passive and take the appropriate actions described above. After you have done that and the crisis has passed, you can safely explore those thoughts from a little distance to better understand what is going on inside you.

Suicidal thinking and suicide attempts are usually indicators that you are suffering and in a lot of psychological pain. Under these difficult conditions, thoughts of suicide usually bubble up as a new idea when your mind has exhausted all other possibilities of finding some relief. Sometimes, it suddenly appears as a new solution. Then, your mind may begin to tell you that suicide is not only a solution but that it's *the* solution. But this is a lie. Suicide is not the solution. It's an answer, but it's not the right one. It's like adding 2 + 2 and getting 5. And then your mind tries to convince you that 5 is not only the right answer but that it's the *only* answer. And then it works on you and works on you until you can't even think of any other answers—just 5 and only 5.

If you slow things down and examine your thoughts more closely, you will discover that your mind is trying to communicate something important about death. If you've been thinking about suicide, then an ending of some kind is indeed being called for, just not yours. Some *thing* is needing to die, not someone.[3] Not you.

If you have suicidal thoughts, then ask yourself, "What is it inside of me that is needing to die?" Think about what is causing you so much distress. What are you holding on to, and why so tightly? What needs to be let go? Is it a way of thinking or seeing things that has to die? Is it a belief about yourself or the world that needs to be given up? For clues, go back and pay close attention to what you were thinking about when your suicidal thoughts began. It can take considerable effort sometimes, but you have the ability to search deeply within yourself and figure out what it is that you need let go of in order to begin to feel better again.

This kind of work can be challenging to do by yourself. Because it can be difficult to have an accurate perspective during these times, work with a trauma-trained therapist to get this thoroughly sorted out for yourself.

So, that's the truth about suicide. Don't get confused. Don't take your thoughts about wanting to die *literally*. Don't let suicidal thinking trick you.

What's true for you?
    Make a list of thoughts and beliefs that are causing you so much pain. What would it take to let each one die? What new thought or belief would take their place? What new things do you need to know about yourself or the world around you?

7

YOUR SUPPORT TEAM

YOU are asked throughout this guide to work in the depths of what happened to you and to get the support you need when you need it. You can avoid much of the long-term suffering experienced after sexual abuse by doing this work and getting support.[1] In this chapter, you will learn how to put together a good support system.

Your team should consist of those people, places, and things that help you feel safe and supported. Team members should have specialties to meet a variety of needs. If possible, and if you need them, get the following types of people, places, and things together to form your system of support:

Therapist with Trauma Training

Choose a therapist with trauma training. Work with someone who makes you feel comfortable. Therapists meet with you as often as needed. Sessions usually last from 45 minutes to an hour. It is common to meet once a week, sometimes more and sometimes less, depending on the circumstances.

Psychiatrist

Psychiatrists are medical doctors with specialized training in mental health who can prescribe medication if needed. They treat people suffering from things like PTSD, anxiety, depression, obsessions, attention deficit disorder (ADD), and sleep issues, to name a few. Once the relationship is established, there is usually a brief meeting every quarter to check how you are doing and how the medication is working. Depending on how severely the sexual abuse is affecting you, working with a psychiatrist may be very beneficial. If you are unsure, work with your therapist to help make that determination.

Psychologist

If you are encountering more severe or persistent problems, sometimes psychological testing is also needed to determine what is happening and why. Psychologists perform these tests and can share the results with your psychiatrist and therapist to help you get the proper treatment. You may only meet with a psychologist a few times to do the evaluation and discuss your results.

School Administrator/Counselor

If you are in high school and struggle from time to time, meet with your principal, vice-principal, dean, or school counselor and let them know of your challenges. They can put in a plan to allow some flexibility to leave class if needed and go to a designated place or person at school for support. If you are in college, go to your campus health center, counseling center, or Title IX office.

Trusted Teacher(s)

If you are a student, let a trusted teacher or advisor know if you struggle in their class or at school. They can work with you to develop some other options in times of distress.

Trusted Friend(s)

It is helpful to talk about your experience with others, but sometimes a trusted friend can be hard to find. Some friends may turn out not to be as trustworthy as you once thought. You may discover closer connections with others who have experienced sexual abuse.

Trusted Co-worker or Boss

Let a trusted co-worker, boss, or human resources person know of your challenges if you struggle at work. They can put plans in place to help you take care of yourself and stay safe at work.

Supportive Caregiver or Family Member(s)

If you have a supportive family member, tell them how you are doing. Ask them to help you set up your team and get the key members in place. If you are a minor, they can assist with communication and coordination with the professionals.

Two Safe Places

First, find a safe place in your mind. Take a few minutes and imagine a scene or a location that feels safe and relaxing for you. The place can be real or imagined. See yourself in that location feeling peaceful and at ease. Breathe deeply and notice how it feels to be there.[2] Go to this safe place in your mind whenever you feel like taking a break.

Next, see if you can find a place in your environment that feels safe. It could be in your room or curled up on a favorite couch or chair, in a library, a cafe, or outside somewhere. Let yourself relax there whenever you can.

Comfort Items

Just like when you were younger, you can still nurture yourself and find comfort with a favorite blanket, stuffed animal, pillow, a favorite article of clothing or hat, a piece of jewelry, a good luck charm, or even a small smooth pebble to hold.[3] Surround yourself with these items. Wear them or carry them with you as often as you like.

Relaxing Activities

Find at least one activity that is usually guaranteed to relax you. Some examples include taking a long shower or hot bath, lighting candles or incense, playing music, taking a walk, playing a game, doing a puzzle, or drawing. What is relaxing for you?

A Place To Put Your Thoughts

In the aftermath of sexual abuse, your mind works overtime. If it is safe and you have some privacy, use a notebook or journal to get your thoughts down on paper. Journaling will help keep thoughts from cycling in your head and is also a way of healing.[4] If you have been keeping your sexual abuse secret, this can be especially hard to do at first.

Websites, Organizations, and Movements

Get connected to websites, organizations, and movements that support those who have been sexually abused. You may find local groups at your school or in your community. Use the internet to connect with websites and larger movements in your state, country, and the world. Draw upon all of them for inspiration and support.

What's true for you?

Look at the different categories of support in this chapter and make a list of what you already have in place. Who or what is missing and needs to be added?

Find an organization at your school, in the community, or online that supports those who have experienced sexual abuse. Challenge yourself to get connected.

8

TRAINING YOUR BRAIN

TENDING the wound of sexual abuse requires patience and skill. Setting an intention to take better care of yourself is a relatively easy thing to do, but accomplishing that goal will be a challenge. (Think about how quickly a New Year's resolution fades.) Because this will take some effort and dedication, you will need *all* parts of your mind working for you and not against you. Neuroscience research shows that only 5% of the brain is used for conscious thinking. The other 95% works unconsciously and out of awareness.[1] So, while your conscious 5% might be saying, "Yes! Let's do this!" your other 95% might not be so excited about it. This chapter teaches you how to work with that other 95% because you will need it to cooperate with you in order to be successful.

How the Other 95% Operates

To get this unconscious 95% part of your brain to cooperate, you first need to understand what motivates it. One of its primary jobs is to stop pain quickly by any means available. Its mission is to provide short-term relief from discomfort. It tries to make you feel good or numb you out, or do both at the same time. This 95% will do anything in the moment to stop pain, *even if it is very harmful for you over time*. Here are some examples of how the 95% operates:

- Feel starved? Overeat.
- Feel bad? Get drunk.
- Feel anxious? Get high.
- Feel alone? Have meaningless sex.

While these things provide temporary relief from suffering, they take a very heavy toll on you physically and psychologically over time. They also create the illusion that you have found quick and easy solutions to your problems. Unfortunately, as you are probably already aware, the pain is still there afterward, just as you left it. Nothing actually gets resolved.[2] Sooner or later, you have to deal with it.[3] If you choose to deal with it now, you will save yourself a lot of misery later on.

Getting the Other 95% On Board

To get that other 95% of your brain on board, it must be trained to work with the goals set by your conscious 5%. Unfortunately, those parts speak different languages, so you will have to talk to the 95% part in its own language. The 5% is logical and rational, whereas the 95% only understands images, bodily sensations, and emotions. Because of this, a picture is worth a thousand words to the 95%.

Create a Vision Board

Use images to create a vision board to communicate directly with your 95%. This messaging will get your 5% and 95% parts on the same page. Images are powerful. They will help you stay clear about your goals and give you a much greater chance of succeeding in your efforts.

Create your vision board by putting together a collage of images, words, poems, song lyrics, magazine pictures, and internet photos that highlight your reasons for wanting to work through all of this. Go back and look at your list of reasons to keep trying that you put together back in Chapter 5 or Appendix C. Find images that are meaningful to you that represent those reasons.

After you have created your vision board and gotten these two parts of the brain on the same page, the best thing you can do to ensure that they keep working together is to take good care of yourself every day, day in and day out. Doing this will help soothe that other 95% and keep it on board and synced up with your longer-term goals.

What's true for you?
Go to Appendix C and look at your reasons to keep trying. (If you didn't do it before, go back and read Chapter 5 and do the exercise.) Find at least one or two images that capture the essence of each reason you listed and create a vision board. If it is safe, put it up where your 95% can see it every day so that it gets the message loud and clear in a language that it can understand.

III

HOW SEXUAL ABUSE
AFFECTS YOU

9

WHAT'S GOING ON INSIDE?

IN this section of the guide, you will learn about how sexual abuse
can affect the mind and body. You will learn how to pay closer
attention to what is going inside of you so that you can organize and
think about your experiences and know what to do about them. This
chapter helps you understand how your mind is working in the
aftermath of sexual abuse and how the abuse may be affecting you. It
also gives you a new way to think about your experiences using a well-
known children's story.

Who Pressed Repeat?

Many people who have experienced sexual abuse find that it can
sometimes be hard to stop thinking about it.[1] It can feel like someone
has pressed the repeat button in your mind, and the memories just

replay over and over for whatever reason. Sometimes, only a particular aspect of the abuse gets repeated. It could be as subtle as a recurring thought, feeling, or sensation.[2] At other times, it can feel as if the whole thing keeps replaying. It is different for everyone. What do you notice about what happens in your mind?

How Sexual Abuse Can Affect You

After experiencing sexual abuse, your survival instincts naturally kick in and start to over-function in an effort to keep you safe.[3] These systems may be working overtime, which can often cause a new set of problems for you. Below is a list of things people can experience after sexual abuse.[4] Check the ones that apply for you.

- ☐ Distracted or underperforming at work
- ☐ Drop in grades or attendance at school
- ☐ Increased anger, rage, or fighting
- ☐ Changing friends or friend groups
- ☐ Hard to get to sleep at night, stay asleep, or get out of bed in the morning
- ☐ Loss of interest in a sport or an activity you used to love
- ☐ Significant weight gain or loss
- ☐ Restricting food intake
- ☐ Binging or purging
- ☐ Hard to concentrate
- ☐ Stomach aches
- ☐ Trying to be perfect or "the best"
- ☐ Problems with bowel movements
- ☐ Recurring dark thoughts
- ☐ Always on guard (hypervigilant)
- ☐ Spiritual crisis or loss of faith
- ☐ Cutting or other problematic self-soothing/self-harming behavior
- ☐ Increase in anxiety or obsessions
- ☐ Hiding negative emotions

☐ Feeling isolated
☐ Doing dangerous or risky things
☐ Increased depression
☐ Increase or decrease in bodily sensations
☐ Increased use of drugs, alcohol, or sex
☐ Feeling flat or numbed out
☐ Increased pressure to excel in school, work, or an activity
☐ Trying to have perfect relationships
☐ Suicidal or murderous thoughts or actions

Try to be gentle with yourself as you look honestly at what is going on for you. It is hard to be curious about yourself while remaining nonjudgmental. Whatever you notice in your situation, be aware that these things can change over time.

At first glance, you might think that these changes have nothing to do with your experience of sexual abuse. But in reality, they are the signs and proof that the abuse actually occurred and is affecting you.[5] Later in Part IV, you will learn how to get these survival instincts calmed back down and let your mind and body know that you are safe now. This will help minimize the types of things listed above and restore you to a sense of well-being more of the time.

Goldilocks and the Three Bears

Even if you have little or no memory of it, sexual abuse can affect you in various ways. Experiences can range from very intense feelings and emotions to complete numbness and disconnection.[6] The children's story "Goldilocks and the Three Bears" provides a way to organize and think about what is going on inside of you. In the story, Goldilocks is hungry and tasting bowls of porridge. One bowl is too hot, another is too cold, but the third one is just right. This story is a reminder for you to notice how you are doing at any given moment.

An essential skill to develop in the aftermath of sexual abuse is figuring out if things inside you are Too Hot, Too Cold, or Just Right. You can do this by taking your emotional temperature many times throughout each day. Pay closer and closer attention to how you are feeling. Especially take note of what it feels like when your moods begin to shift. Notice what was going on or what you were thinking *just before* things started to change. Make a habit of paying attention in this way. It helps you get good at noticing when you are becoming Too Hot or Too Cold. Importantly, you will also notice those times when you are feeling Just Right. Some people only become Too Hot or Too Cold in the aftermath of sexual abuse, but others can feel both simultaneously.[7] It can be a lot to sort out.

When hard memories or intense bodily sensations come, sometimes without much warning, you can become Too Hot or Too Cold very quickly, sometimes even before you notice it. So, pay attention to what happens in your mind and with your body. Notice your breathing and any bodily sensations. These are the ways in which your mind and body remember what happened and are now trying to keep you safe.[8] These Too Hot and Too Cold states are explored more closely in the following two chapters so that you can more clearly understand how the wound of sexual abuse may be affecting you.

What's true for you?

How do you think your experience of sexual abuse is affecting you now? If you did not do it already, go back and look at the list in this chapter and check any boxes that apply. What other experiences have you had that are not on the list?

Do you know what you are feeling or how you are doing at any given moment? Take your emotional temperature right now by asking yourself, "What is going on inside of me," "What am I feeling right now," and "Am I Too Hot, Too Cold, or Just Right?"

10

TOO HOT

MANY people have the experience of getting Too Hot in the aftermath of sexual abuse.[1] Becoming Too Hot is also known as *hyperarousal*. This is the brain's "fight or flight" response when danger is perceived. It tries to keep you safe by urging you to either attack or run away. Because sexual abuse is so intense, the traumatic memories of it get stored in a more primitive part of the brain.[2] When re-activated, it can feel as if the sexual abuse is happening all over again or is about to. PTSD studies show that neurons in your brain fire the same way whether the sexual abuse is actually occurring or you are just reliving a traumatic memory.[3] So, things can get Too Hot in a hurry and feel very real.

Getting Too Hot can look a little different for everyone. Think about your experience of sexual abuse and read the following statements describing what it feels like when getting Too Hot. Check the ones that apply for you.

- ☐ I feel tense.
- ☐ My body starts to shake.
- ☐ I get emotional.
- ☐ I get defensive.
- ☐ My hands (or other body parts) tremble.
- ☐ My throat tightens. My voice gets shaky.
- ☐ I get sweaty.
- ☐ My stomach starts to hurt.
- ☐ I feel trapped.
- ☐ My face gets red.
- ☐ My mind starts racing. I can't concentrate.
- ☐ I get flashbacks of images that are hard to put out of my mind.
- ☐ I feel overwhelmed.
- ☐ I get scared.
- ☐ I get a headache.
- ☐ I urgently have to use the restroom.
- ☐ I want to get up and move.
- ☐ I feel like I am crawling out of my skin.
- ☐ I can't catch my breath.
- ☐ I feel unsafe or like something bad is going to happen again.
- ☐ I obsess. I can't quit thinking about bad stuff.
- ☐ I am on guard and can't relax.
- ☐ I get really angry or even full of rage sometimes.
- ☐ I want to holler and scream or get violent.
- ☐ I get sad, and I cry.
- ☐ I leave or want to run away.
- ☐ My heart pounds, and I can't slow it down.

Are there others that happen to you that are not on this list? These are all signs that the memories of your sexual abuse are affecting you and may be traumatic. Chapters 19 and 20 deal specifically with PTSD symptoms and provide guidance on what to do if you experience them.

Sometimes, in the beginning, it can be hard to figure out what is causing you to become Too Hot. It takes time to develop emotional awareness. For now, it is important to identify what is actually happening inside of you and make the connections to your abuse. With time and practice, you will figure out what types of things and situations cause you to become Too Hot. You may have some notions already.

What's true for you?
What does it feel like for you when you get Too Hot?

Can you think of some people, places, or situations that cause you to become Too Hot?

II

Too Cold

INSTEAD of getting Too Hot in the aftermath of sexual abuse, some people have the opposite experience and become Too Cold.[1] This is called *hypoarousal* and is the brain's "freeze" response. When grave danger is perceived, the oldest part of the brain gets activated. It automatically tries to create safety by causing the body to freeze and play dead, hoping that the danger will pass.[2] Just like getting Too Hot, this is also a natural and normal response when under great duress.

Think about your experience of sexual abuse and look at the following list of statements describing what it can feel like to become Too Cold. Check any that apply for you.

- ☐ I feel numb. I can't feel anything.
- ☐ It's like I leave my body.
- ☐ I don't feel present.
- ☐ Parts of me don't feel present.
- ☐ I feel frozen.
- ☐ I can't defend myself. I am helpless.
- ☐ I feel weak or passive.
- ☐ Things feel dreamlike.
- ☐ I can't think. My mind goes blank.
- ☐ I feel disconnected.
- ☐ I feel ashamed.
- ☐ I can't find my voice.
- ☐ I have no energy.
- ☐ I feel grayed out, flat, or lifeless.
- ☐ I feel dead.
- ☐ I go foggy.
- ☐ Things don't feel real.
- ☐ I shut down.
- ☐ I can't say no.
- ☐ I feel really small or invisible.
- ☐ I disappear or go somewhere else in my mind.

Are there others that happen for you that are not on this list? These Too Cold feelings and sensations are signs that your sexual abuse is affecting you and may be traumatic. See Chapter 19 for more information on PTSD and what to do about it.

Automatic Responses

We are biologically wired with three options: fight, flight, or freeze when we get overwhelmed. These Too Hot and Too Cold reactions are all innate attempts at self-protection.[3] It is important to know that you don't have control over which of these three survival instincts will kick in and when.[4] Sometimes, in the aftermath of sexual abuse, these fight, flight, or freeze instincts can even get activated while you are sleeping and having an intense dream.[5]

Think about your experience of sexual abuse. Which of these three survival instincts kicked in for you? If you don't like how your mind and body responded, try to avoid judging yourself harshly. Whether you fought back, tried to run away, or froze, know that this was your mind and body reacting automatically on instinctual levels to try and protect you.

What's true for you?

What does it feel like for you when you become Too Cold?

Can you think of some people, places, or situations that cause you to become Too Cold?

If you are critical of how your mind or body reacted while you were being sexually abused, what can you tell yourself that would be less judgmental?

12

GETTING JUST RIGHT

GIVEN a chance to properly heal, the mind has an astonishing capacity and determination to get itself re-regulated.[1] In the previous two chapters, you learned what happens when things get Too Hot or Too Cold. This chapter helps you identify what it feels like when things are regulated and feel Just Right for you. It is very important to recognize what it feels like when you are doing well and reinforce those feelings. In the aftermath of sexual abuse, people describe their sense of being able to stay Just Right like this:

- It feels like I have choices about what to do or how to react.
- I am able to stay in my body.
- I feel OK in my body.
- I am able to stay in the moment.

- I stay open and curious.
- I stay aware of boundaries, both mine and others.
- I am aware that I have choices.
- I stay aware of my feelings and can still think at the same time.
- My reactions seem OK for the situation.
- I can watch the feeling or memory come and not get too wrapped up in it. I can watch it pass.
- I notice my breathing speeding up and my heart beating faster, but I can stay with them as they slow back down.
- I can tolerate my feelings even when they are very strong.
- I am able to stay in class and do my classwork.
- I can do my homework.
- I can think and concentrate.
- I feel like I have control over my body.
- I feel in control of the situation.
- I am able to communicate what I'm experiencing to loved ones safely and calmly.
- I am able to stay at work and continue doing my job.
- I can remember and practice self-soothing exercises if I need to.
- I am able to say what I'm feeling, either aloud or within myself.
- I am aware that I am physically present and safe now.
- I can perform my day-to-day tasks.
- I am able to use my voice.
- I feel as though I am "watching" the memory, not participating in it or reliving it.
- I can be in situations that are emotionally hard for me and be OK.
- I am aware that I have choices, and I can leave situations that make me feel uncomfortable or unsafe.

Before your sexual abuse occurred, you probably did many of these things quite naturally without ever thinking about them. Now, you might notice that it is harder to keep yourself feeling Just Right.[2] You may also find yourself alternating between feeling Too Hot and Too

Cold in an effort to stay safe and deal with the trauma.[3] As you work through this guide and work with your trauma-trained therapist, you should begin to notice yourself spending more and more time feeling Just Right. This means you are making real progress at learning how to tend your wound properly. Be patient with yourself. This takes time.

Everyone experiences some version of getting Too Hot or Too Cold. Because sexual abuse has a big impact, you may now have big versions of this stuff. Therefore, you will now need some Big Skills to bring yourself back to feeling Just Right. The next section of this guide will teach you those skills and show you how to get your mind and body calmed back down so that you feel stable and good about yourself more of the time.

What's true for you?

Picture yourself in a situation from the past where you have become Too Hot or Too Cold. Now, in your mind's eye, see yourself allowing the hotness or coolness to wash over you and then letting it pass. See yourself returning to Just Right again. Take a moment and practice this in your mind right now.

Think about a recent situation where you stayed Just Right when you usually would become Too Hot or Too Cold. Review the list above and check the boxes that applied for you in this instance.

IV

GETTING CALM AND STABLE

13

LEAN IN TO DISCOMFORT

I N the aftermath of sexual abuse, even ordinary everyday upsets can sometimes become much more intense.[1] For example, a little nervousness can now lead to anxiety and panic, whereas it didn't before. Or an irritation can quickly turn into anger and rage. After becoming Too Hot or Too Cold, getting yourself back to Just Right may now take more conscious effort and skill than it did before. Because these more intense feelings are harder to tolerate, you will learn a new technique in this chapter to help manage through them. Rather than trying to avoid or ignore them, you will be learning how to *lean in* and get curious about them.[2]

Instead of trying to push them away, begin to practice leaning in and going *toward* your intense thoughts, feelings, and emotions.[3] Go ahead and allow them to come, and try and feel them as fully as possible. Get curious about your experience by paying very close attention to what is happening inside. In addition to your thoughts, notice what you are feeling and what sensations you are having in your body. As you notice, don't make judgments about yourself. *Stay curious.* Just keep noticing and noticing . . . and noticing.

For example, if you find yourself getting anxious, instead of trying to avoid the discomfort, you can choose to do something very different. You can choose to stay right with the feeling of anxiety itself. Allowing it to come and staying present with it is the best and most direct way of dealing with it.[4] Try to become the *curious observer* of how these particular anxious feelings in this specific moment are moving through you.[5] Notice what it feels like inside you as the anxiety intensifies. Notice what is going on in your body: notice your breathing, your heartbeat, and the sensations you are having. Notice the thoughts and images that come to mind. Then notice what happens as the intensity starts to lessen and begins to pass. And finally, notice what it feels like as you return to feeling Just Right again. Then congratulate yourself because you have just weathered a great storm, and you have been right there with yourself all the way through it!

If you deal with your intense emotional states in this way, there will be less self-criticism and acting out, and you will feel much better about yourself. Train yourself to lean in and be your own best and most curious observer. Over and over every day, practice observing without judging. Like the other skills in this guide, this takes practice and can be used over a lifetime. This technique is powerful, proven, and it works. Later in Chapter 17, you will work at an even deeper level in the effort to free yourself from whatever is causing so much distress. Practice leaning in and staying curious from now on. This will be the strong foundation from which you will work later on.

Get Additional Support If Needed

Regardless of the skills used, sometimes people cannot get their systems re-regulated and spend much of their time in distressing emotional states. If this is happening for you, you will need additional support. If you do not have a psychiatrist on your support team (see Chapter 7), you may need to add one and let them know what you are experiencing. They can prescribe medication that can help stabilize your system while you learn these calming skills.

What's true for you?

Think about something that gets you activated. Invite those feelings or emotions to come forward. You may not get the full intensity, but you might get enough to practice the skills outlined above. Lean in and get curious. Feel it intensify and then begin to lessen. Watch it pass and feel yourself return to Just Right again.

14

BREATHE

A FTER learning how to lean in and get curious about whatever is happening inside you, you will also want to learn how to interrupt your Too Hot and Too Cold cycles. The following three chapters introduce those skills. In this chapter, you will discover the power of your own breath to help regulate yourself in the face of any emotional state or circumstance.

Breathing has been studied for thousands of years, and many different techniques have been developed over the centuries.[1] Breathing has always been our first and most powerful tool. One primary way to stay regulated is by taking nice easy, full belly breaths. However, in the aftermath of sexual abuse, breathing can often become quite shallow and irregular.[2]

This chapter introduces two very simple but powerful breathing practices that will (1) increase awareness of your breathing, (2) retrain you to take fuller inhales and exhales again, (3) reconnect you to your body, (4) refocus the mind, and (5) help restore a sense of calm.[3] When you become Too Hot or Too Cold, these are the fastest, most direct, and most effective ways to get back to feeling Just Right again. Allow yourself to try each technique as you read the instructions below.

Seven Belly Breaths

1. *Notice Your Breathing*

    Place one hand on your chest and the other on your belly. Without changing anything, just notice your breath. Are you breathing only up in the chest, or are you getting air down into the belly? Are you breathing through your nose or mouth? Is your breathing shallow or deep? Fast or slow?

    Becoming aware of how you are breathing is an essential first step. It sounds easy, but it can be pretty challenging. What are you noticing as you try it? It is hard to accept your breathing as it is. (Even harder to accept ourselves as we are!) It is hard not to change it once you become aware.

2. *Take Seven Belly Breaths*

    If you feel comfortable, close your mouth and breathe through your nose if you can. You will be taking seven belly breaths while counting to yourself the whole time. A belly breath happens when you inhale and pull air down into the bottom of your lungs, and your belly rises. Then, as you exhale, push all the air out of the lungs while letting your belly sink back down. Practice this a few times to get a feel for it. See the belly rise as you inhale and fall as you exhale. Overexaggerate the belly rising and falling to get a good feel for how to get the air deep down into your lungs.

    When you are ready, start the exercise by exhaling completely. Push all the air out. Next, inhale slowly and deeply, pulling the air down into your belly while counting in your mind, "One, one, one,

one, one . . ." the whole time during the inhale. If you can, look down and watch the hand on your belly rise as your lower lungs fill with air.

Once your belly is full of air, slowly exhale while continuing to count "One, one, one, one, one . . ." in your mind. While repeating the number silently to yourself, imagine the shape of that number in your mind. See the number "1" in your mind while repeating, "One, one, one . . ." all the way through the inhale *and* exhale.

On the second breath, count to yourself, "Two, two, two, two, two . . ." all the way through the inhale and exhale while also seeing the number 2 in your mind. And so on. **Repeat seven times.**

3. *Repeat if Needed*

If you still feel Too Hot or Too Cold after doing a round of Seven Belly Breaths, then do another round. Begin again at number one. Sometimes an extra round (or two) is needed to get back to feeling Just Right. Remember to count in your mind as you go and visualize the numbers. This is as important as the breathing.

4. *Finish*

To finish, take a nice deep belly breath in, hold it for a second or two, then exhale completely, and *just let it all go.* Notice how you feel.

While doing Seven Belly Breaths, you may notice the exhales getting longer. You might even notice a natural pause at the end of the exhale. Let your body start the next inhale whenever it wants to. Don't force it. You may feel your body beginning to relax. You may feel more connected to yourself. Whatever you had been thinking about may have also passed because the only things you have been thinking about and imagining are ones, twos, threes, fours, fives, sixes, and sevens. If the intense thoughts, feelings, or sensations return, then repeat Seven

Belly Breaths as often as necessary. When you finish your seventh breath, if you are feeling relaxed, shift your attention to your breathing and just notice the air flowing in and out. Notice how this feels.

You might have the opposite experience and find it difficult at times to get all the way to seven while breathing, counting, and imagining. Your mind may wander off to other things. It can take some concentrated effort to simultaneously breathe, count, and imagine all at the same time. If your mind wanders, simply start over again. Be patient with yourself. You may be surprised to discover just how quickly your mind works! Gently keep bringing your mind back to the beginning as many times as needed to complete the exercise.

The exercise above looks simple, and you might be thinking that it is a waste of time or would never work for you. But don't be fooled! This "simple" breathing technique is over two thousand years old.[4] It is time time-tested and very effective. With a little practice, you can easily master it.

However, even if you learn and practice this breathing technique, it can still be hard to remember to do it—especially when you get overwhelmed. If you find that this is happening for you, then try the simpler Three Breaths exercise described below.[5]

Three Breaths

First, stop whatever you are doing and pay attention to your physical sensations. Now, take three breaths. That's it! It is that simple. Three inhales and three exhales. Go ahead and try it now. It only takes a few seconds. Three Breaths is a powerful way to bring yourself back into the moment and help stop the cycling in your head about the past or the future.

When to do Breathing Exercises

You can do a breathing exercise anytime and anywhere. You can do one standing, seated, or lying down. In public, if you are seated, just rest a hand casually in your lap and breathe that way. Do a breathing exercise whenever you feel anxious or afraid. Do one anytime you get Too Hot or Too Cold. If you drive, do one while waiting at a red light. Do one of the exercises at bedtime if you find it hard to sleep at night, first thing in the morning if your mind starts to race, or in the middle of the night if you wake up and can't get back to sleep. You can also do one before or during important meetings, exams, athletic events, or performances. They are also great to do whenever you find yourself in situations where you are dealing with people in power and whenever you feel intimidated, controlled, or attacked. Do one anytime there is emotional turmoil.

Appendix D has a wallet-sized copy of these techniques. Cut it out and keep it with you. If you have a phone, take a picture, and store it as a reminder just in case you forget what to do when you get overwhelmed.

Caution

Recovering from sexual abuse is about learning how to take good care of yourself and remembering to do it over and over again. Because your breathing may be affected, doing any breathing exercise may be scary at first. Remember, you have choices. Allow yourself to do these exercises in whatever way feels best and safest. For example, if full belly breaths are uncomfortable, try inhaling or exhaling only just a little more deeply. Even a subtle change like this can make a real difference in how you feel.

What's true for you?
Full belly breaths are very different from big chest breaths. Only belly breaths relax and calm. Experiment with both to feel the difference. Practice *belly* breathing until you are doing it most of the time!

Next time you feel anxious, scared, angry, or numb, do Seven Belly Breaths. Notice how you feel afterward.

15

BODY CHECKS

THE experience of sexual abuse can cause you to feel disconnected from yourself or from specific parts of your body.[1] Like the Too Hot and Too Cold reactions described in earlier chapters, this is also a natural defense. In the previous chapter, you learned how to pay closer attention to your breathing using the Seven Belly Breaths and Three Breaths techniques. In this chapter, you will learn how to do Body Checks to help you further reconnect with your body.

You can do the Body Check exercise described below whenever you get Too Hot or Too Cold. It will help bring you back to feeling Just Right again. Like the breathing exercises, Body Checks are fast and effective. If you feel comfortable, allow yourself to try it as you read through it.

Body Check

1. Begin by wiggling your toes. Notice the balls of your feet, your arches, and your heels.
2. Bring awareness to both legs. Tense all the muscles in both legs, hold for 5 seconds and then relax. Repeat 3 times.
3. Notice your buttocks and how they are supported. Shift your weight slightly from side to side and notice how that feels.
4. Next, bring awareness to your back. Notice where it makes contact with the surface supporting it and where it doesn't.
5. Now move your head from side to side and gently all around. Open and close your mouth. Move your jaw around and let go of any tension.
6. Bring awareness to your hands. Slowly make fists. Tense all the muscles in both arms, hold for 5 seconds and then relax. Repeat 3 times.
7. Now focus on just one hand. Rub one of your fingers with your thumb. Notice how that feels on your finger. Switch perspectives and rub your thumb with that same finger. Notice how that feels on your thumb.
8. Repeat using your other hand.
9. Notice any changes in how you are feeling.
10. Repeat this exercise if you still feel disconnected.

Like the breathing exercises from the previous chapter, this exercise may also look simple, but it, too, is powerful and proven. Safely and gently, it invites you back into your body again and helps you get reconnected with yourself.

When to do Body Checks

You can do a Body Check almost anytime and anywhere. Do it when you get Too Hot or Too Cold. Do a portion of it whenever you like. Do it at bedtime to help you relax. Body Checks are great to do whenever things feel chaotic inside, or you feel disconnected, numb, anxious, angry, stressed, or intimidated.

Appendix D has a wallet-sized copy of this exercise. Cut it out and keep it with you. If you have a cell phone, take a picture, and store it as a reminder.

Caution

Recovering from sexual abuse is about learning to take good care of yourself. Remember that you always have choices. At first, you may find it hard to reconnect with feelings or sensations in your body. This can take time. Go slow and just be where you are. Ease off if the feelings or sensations become too intense.

Allow yourself to do this exercise in whatever way feels best and safest for you. Any awareness, however slight, is very beneficial. Do not force anything. Modify the Body Check in ways that feel most comfortable for you. For example, you might decide just to feel your feet on the floor or rub your finger and thumb and then choose to stop. You have control now. You get to decide what works best for you.

Practice breathing and body checks over and over again every day. They are fast, effective, free, and always available. Reconnect with your breath and body as often as you can. This is how you tend the wound of your sexual abuse and promote healing. Teaching yourself how to breathe deeply again and being fully in your body is restorative.[2] These are the foundations for a lifetime of well-being.

What's true for you?

Do you feel disconnected from yourself or parts of your body from time to time?

If you didn't do a Body Check while reading along, go back now and give it a try if you can. If you did do one, try it again, time it, and see how long it takes. Notice how you feel afterward.

Next, try doing a Body Check followed by either Three Breaths or Seven Belly Breaths. Time it and see how long it takes to do both. Notice how you feel afterward.

16

MORE BIG SKILLS

I N the previous two chapters, you learned two valuable breathing techniques and how to do Body Checks. Continue practicing them over and over every day until they become second nature for you. This chapter introduces more Big Skills that you can use to help get calm and stable. These may require more time and space and the ability to get up and move around. Some may have a cost associated with them. In the aftermath of sexual abuse, it is important to do things for yourself that calm the mind, reconnect you to your body, and invite healing. Here are some other Big Skills that you can try:

Get Moving

If either your fight/flight or freeze response has been activated, work with it if you can. Get yourself moving. Go up and down a flight of stairs, or go for a walk, jog, or run. It doesn't have to be very far. Even a walk to the end of a block or around a school or work building can be beneficial.

You can also do some jumping jacks if you are able. Let the adrenaline flow and get your heart rate up. Shake out your arms and legs. Move your head gently all around. Play some music and start dancing.[1] Get the energy moving in your body.

Writing/Drawing

If your mind is running, put your thoughts down on paper. This can help slow things down in your head. The act of writing is also a way of healing.[2] It causes you to think about your thoughts and begin to understand them. Also, you can draw or paint any images or feelings that come to mind.[3]

Yoga/Tai-Chi/Qi Gong

Anything that invites self-awareness is very beneficial in the aftermath of sexual abuse.[4] The mind-body practices of yoga, Tai-Chi, and Qi Gong are gaining popularity. Find a trauma-sensitive yoga class locally or online if you are able. If you feel comfortable, let instructors know a little bit about you, so they can provide additional support along the way if needed. With online classes, you can practice in the privacy of your own space if that works better for you.

When trying these activities, it is normal to experience uneasiness at first. Be patient and keep at it. Research shows that real and lasting change comes after about 20 weeks of consistent practice.[5] It takes time to re-wire things and get your mind and body fully relaxed and completely calmed down again.

Meditation/Mindfulness

Meditation and mindfulness practices are also effective in tending the wound of sexual abuse.[6] Look for programs or groups at your school, in your community, or online. There are plenty of resources online for beginners.[7] You can practice at home using websites, videos, or apps that assist with learning how to meditate and develop mindfulness. As with other mind/body practices, they may be challenging to do at first, and you will need to consistently practice for at least 20 weeks in order to re-wire your brain and create lasting change.

What's true for you?
Which Big Skills listed in this chapter are you interested in trying?

Is there something not on this list that came to mind that you want to explore?

Can you allow yourself to give them a try?

V

GOING DEEPER

17

STRONG EMOTIONS AND INNER CRITICS

IN earlier sections, you learned how to identify and tolerate strong emotions and bodily sensations in order to re-regulate and get back to feeling Just Right. The skill it takes to manage internal storms and calm yourself is hard-won. However, actually freeing yourself from ongoing inner turmoil requires that you work at an even deeper level. This section teaches you how to do that. In this chapter, you will learn how to work at that deeper level by using *imaginal dialogues*.[1] This powerful technique will help you deal directly with strong emotions, numbness, nightmares, or any inner critics that cause distress.

If you pay attention to what is going on in your mind, you may notice that there is often some sort of inner dialogue taking place between different parts of ourselves. (For example, one part of you might want to wake up early while another part would rather sleep late. These two parts or "voices" then engage in an internal struggle to determine what happens.) Inner conversations about things large and small are natural for everyone. However, just like with feelings and emotions, these inner dialogues can become much more intense now in the aftermath of sexual abuse. If left unchecked, they can become oppressive, extremely harsh, overly critical, or even frightening. So, you will need to learn to use your imagination, a most powerful tool, in an active and purposeful way to have imaginal dialogues with these disturbing emotions and inner critics. This will help you get to their core, deal with them, and free yourself from the discomfort.

Caution

If you have not done so already, read the previous chapters in this guide and complete the exercises before moving forward. You will need those skills to do this work safely and confidently. The chapters in this section are concerned with the most intense aspects of sexual abuse. They focus on the core of the wound. Also, as mentioned throughout this guide, *get the support you need.* It is strongly recommended that you work with a trauma-trained therapist if possible. Seek help immediately if this work becomes overwhelming. Remember that you always have choices. Ease off or stop anytime things begin to feel too intense.

Imaginal Dialogues

Imaginal dialogues are used to work with strong emotions and inner critics that are already present inside and possess some energy.[2] This work is very different from "imaginary" fantasizing, which is more of a fanciful "making things up." When used correctly, imaginal dialogues help ease tensions in the mind, stop the inner battles, and provide some much-needed inner relief and peace.

In Chapter 13, you learned how to lean in and stay curious about whatever is happening inside of you. To have an imaginal dialogue with whatever is causing distress, you will need to stay with it long enough to allow for an inner image to arise without chasing it away or overly fixating on it.[3] For example, if you are working with an inner voice that is judging and critical of you, lean in and invite that voice to become embodied in your mind. Differentiate it. This may take courage. Ask the voice to take a shape and become an inner figure or image. Notice what shape the voice takes. What or who does it become? Allow the image to exist in your mind if you are able. Then you can work with it. Sometimes, it can take a little while for an image to arise, so be patient. You will be engaging in an imaginal dialogue with this image, so see if you can let it enliven a bit and let it communicate for itself.

Below are the instructions for how to have an imaginal dialogue. To get some practice, choose something to work with that has been causing you some inner distress, whether it be a strong emotion or an inner critic. Write down your responses to the following prompts on a piece of paper.

Imaginal Dialogue

- When thinking about this inner critic, voice, feeling, or emotion, what image comes to mind? Draw the image. Write a description of it with as much detail as you can. Get specific. This is your image of it. Today. Right now. Pause in your mind and ask these questions: What does it look like? Is it animate or inanimate? Does it have a shape? Is it hard or soft? Does it have edges? What color is it? Is it big or small? Young or old? Does it have a name? And so on.

- Describe what it feels like to you.

- Where is it in your body? Put your hands on those parts. What happens if you breathe into those parts?

- Describe how it sounds.

- Now, speak with the image. Ask it to talk. Let it say what it wants to say. Write down whatever it says.

- Respond to what the image said. Talk to it. Tell it whatever comes to mind. Write down your response.

- Don't banish the image, and don't run away from it. Stay curious if you can. Continuing talking back and forth with it.

Ask it, "Why are you here now," and "What do you want to say?" Listen for the responses and write down what it says.

- Keep the conversation going. Write down what each of you says. Keep asking it questions. Tell the image what you want it to know. Listen to its responses.
- Write down your imaginal dialogue as it unfolds.

You can also engage with the image in other ways. For example, make a movement or get into a position that shows what this image feels like to you. Then make a movement or position your body in response. Continue moving, back and forth, just as in the conversation.

When doing an imaginal dialogue, pay attention to what happens with the emotion, feeling, or inner figure. It may morph from one thing into another. Your relationship with it may change. Whatever happens, let it shift and evolve. Write down or draw any changes. Notice any shifts in how you feel or think as you do this work.

Remember that feelings, emotions, and inner figures are emerging and receding all the time in our minds. They have their own unique way of communicating with us and affecting us. Imaginal dialogues can be used with anyone or anything—real or not, living or dead. Slow things down in your mind and learn to work with them instead of trying to ignore them. This will go a long way in your effort to tend the wound of sexual abuse. In Appendix E, there is a list of these step-by-step instructions for doing imaginal dialogues.

What's true for you?
Is there an emotion, internal voice, or figure in your mind that you are always wrestling with or that "haunts" you? If so, have an imaginal dialogue with it using the questions in Appendix E.

18

NUMBNESS

SOME people who have experienced sexual abuse do not get overwhelmed with strong feelings and emotions or have harsh inner critics. Instead, they experience something altogether different. They may go numb or have a vague sense of feeling disconnected.[1] Some people experience both numbness and strong emotions. Numbing is one way that the mind protects you from uncomfortable feelings, sensations, and emotions connected to your sexual abuse.[2] Sometimes, you may only feel numb in one area of your body (or your life) but have strong feelings or emotions in other areas. It is different for everyone. Because numbness impairs your ability to properly tend the wound of sexual abuse, you will learn how to work directly with it in this chapter.

If you experience numbness, you may find yourself acting out in various ways in an attempt to get yourself to feel something—anything.

This can lead down dangerous and self-destructive paths. If this is the case for you, then reconnecting with your body, thoughts, feelings, sensations, intuitions, and emotions is crucial.

Leaning In to Numbness

To work with numbness, take a moment to recognize and acknowledge that you are actually feeling numb and disconnected. Next, lean in and go toward the numbness by asking yourself: "But what am I *really* feeling right now," "Where do I feel it in my body," and "What does it feel like?" Become the curious observer and see what you notice. If nothing comes, ask: "If I *could* feel something, what is it that I would be feeling?" Even if nothing comes, keep asking yourself these questions every day until you begin to get some answers. You are planting seeds and watering them with your repeated questioning. Reconnection can take some time.

When you do begin to feel something, it may be hard to describe at first. Many just notice a slight discomfort or an uneasy feeling. If this happens for you, notice where you feel it in your body. Stay with it if you can. This is a great start!

Leaning in and moving toward the numbness related to sexual abuse can be scary because you may start to have thoughts, feelings, or sensations connected to what happened. As you find your own emotional and feeling scales again, use the list of questions below to help you stay curious and not get overwhelmed. After being numb, anything can be hard to tolerate at first, so go slowly with yourself.

Imaginal Dialogues with Numbness

Imaginal dialogues, the same technique you learned in the previous chapter, can be used effectively to deal with numbness.[3] If you or a part of you feels numb or disconnected, then do this exercise. Respond to the following prompts. Write your answers on a piece of paper.

- How numb do you feel on a scale of 1 to 10, with 1 being completely present and 10 being completely numbed out?

74

- Where in your body do you feel most numb? Put your hands on those parts.
- What does your numbness feel like?
- What does your numbness look like? Does it have a shape? If so, what shape? Is it hard or soft? Does it have edges? What color is it?
- What image comes to mind when thinking about this numbness? Draw a picture of it.
- Does your numbness have a sound? If so, let yourself make that sound.
- If your numbness could speak, what would it say? How would it say it, and to whom? Write it down. Say it out loud.
- Talk to your numbness. Ask it, "Why are you here now," and "What do you want me to know?" Listen for a response and write down what it says.
- Keep the conversation going back and forth. Ask it questions. Tell it what you want it to know. Listen to its responses. Write down what you say to one another as your imaginal dialogue unfolds.
- To finish, return your hand to the place that most holds the numbness. Direct your breath toward that spot. Breath into it for a moment or two. What do you notice? What happens?

You can also engage with your numbness in other ways. For example, you can make a movement or get into a position that expresses this numbness. Also, is there a poem or song that comes to mind that captures this feeling of numbness? Read the poem aloud or play the music and sing along.

You can have an imaginal dialogue with numbness any time you like. Appendix E has a list of these prompts to help guide you. You may notice emotions or feelings starting to come up and get stronger when doing this work. They may morph from one thing into another. Your relationship with them may change over time. Let it shift and evolve. It is OK to let yourself know what you know and feel what you feel.

Remember, feelings and emotions are emerging all the time. They have their own unique way of communicating with you. Numbing is a way of blocking those important communications. Learning to allow them to come up again involves overriding the automatic disconnect that has gotten set up. Working through numbness is another important step along the way in learning to tend the wound of sexual abuse.

What's true for you?
Have an imaginal dialogue with your feeling of numbness using the prompts in this chapter or Appendix E.

19

"Big T" Trauma

THE previous chapters in this guide have helped you figure out how sexual abuse may be affecting you and have taught you how to tolerate and manage when things get Too Hot or Too Cold. You have also learned how to get to the core of strong emotions, deal with inner critics, and work through numbness. In this chapter, you will learn about posttraumatic stress disorder (PTSD), whether or not you may have it, and if so, what you can do about it.

This chapter does not appear earlier in the guide because, whether or not you meet the criteria for PTSD, you still need the other skills introduced thus far to properly tend the wound of sexual abuse. Use the information in this chapter to think about your experience with a more informed perspective and in a larger context. Your knowledge and insight are powerful.

"Big T" Trauma

The mental health professions divide trauma into two broad categories: "Big T" Trauma and "little t" trauma.[1] Sexual abuse is classified as a Big T Trauma and includes physical abuse, war, severe car accidents, or natural disasters. Little t trauma, also known as developmental trauma, includes things like non-life-threatening injuries, being bullied or disciplined at school, the death of a pet, parents separating, or emotional abuse.

Both types of trauma have the potential to be psychologically devastating. People can develop PTSD from Big T Trauma or little t trauma. This chapter includes lists of PTSD symptoms that can emerge in the aftermath of sexual abuse. These lists are adapted from the manual that doctors and therapists use to make PTSD diagnoses.[2] Only trained professionals can formally diagnose. However, it can be helpful to think whether the aftereffects of your sexual abuse might meet the criteria for PTSD. And if so, what you can do about it.

Posttraumatic Stress Disorder (PTSD)

Having one or more of the following symptoms *for more than one month* could be an indicator of PTSD. Check any that you have experienced for more than one month.

- ☐ Upsetting memories of the sexual abuse keep coming back, popping into your head, or will not go away.
- ☐ Having bad dreams related to the sexual abuse.
- ☐ Flashbacks where it feels like it is happening all over again.
- ☐ Getting really upset by reminders or symbols of the abuse.
- ☐ Strong desire to avoid memories, thoughts, or feelings about or related to the abuse.
- ☐ Strong desire to avoid whatever reminds you of the sexual abuse, such as certain people, places, activities, objects, or conversations.
- ☐ Can't remember an important part or parts of the sexual abuse.

☐ Continuous overly negative thoughts like, "I am bad," "No one can be trusted," "The world is completely dangerous," or "I am permanently ruined."

☐ Continually thinking about the cause or consequences of your sexual abuse where you blame yourself or others.

☐ Being stuck in a negative emotional state such as fear, horror, anger, guilt, or shame.

☐ No longer having an interest in or quitting things you used to like.

☐ Feeling detached, isolated, or cut off from others.

☐ Hard to experience positive emotions like happiness, joy, satisfaction, or loving feelings.

Having two or more of the following symptoms could be an indicator of PTSD. Check any that you have experienced *for more than one month*.

☐ Aggressive behavior or angry outbursts for little or no reason.

☐ Reckless or self-destructive behavior.

☐ Always being on guard (hypervigilance).

☐ Exaggerated startle response.

☐ Problems concentrating.

☐ Troubles with sleep: difficulty falling asleep, problems staying asleep, or restless sleep.

A PTSD diagnosis requires that you have the symptom(s) in the above lists for more than one month *and* that you have them to the degree that it is hard to function at work, school, home, or with friends. With PTSD, things can also feel unreal at times. Check either or both of the following if they apply for you.

☐ You often do not feel real, or it feels like time moves slowly.

☐ The world around you often does not feel real or feels dreamlike, distant, or distorted.

PTSD also has other descriptors. These lists provide an idea of what some people experience after a Big T Trauma like sexual abuse. Do not get worried if you checked multiple boxes on these lists. Trauma expresses itself in numerous ways. Just like your body, your mind has also been violated, and it is doing all sorts of things right now to try and process what happened and keep you safe.

Get Support

If you have symptoms indicative of PTSD, then get support from a trauma-trained therapist. They can properly diagnose, provide an appropriate course of treatment, and work with you to alleviate these symptoms. If you are suffering, have some compassion for yourself and get the support you need and deserve.

What's true for you?
How did you feel reading the lists of symptoms in this chapter and thinking about PTSD?

What other "Big T" and "little t" traumas have you experienced?

20

Triggers and Flashbacks

GETTING triggered and having flashbacks can be common after sexual abuse and are indicators of PTSD.[1] This chapter teaches you how to identify triggers and provides guidance on what to do if you have flashbacks about your abuse.

Triggers

A *trigger* is anything that re-activates traumatic memories that have been stored in a more primitive part of the brain.[2] They cause you to become Too Hot or Too Cold, and they can cause flashbacks. However, a trigger does not always cause a flashback. Sometimes, a trigger only causes you to have the experience of getting Too Hot or Too Cold.

There are all kinds of triggers, and they can be different for each person. They also can change over time. Some common triggers include

- seeing the person or people who violated you,
- being in the same place or near where the violation happened,
- smelling something that reminds you of the abuse,
- seeing a scene in a movie or show,
- hearing news of other sexual abuse incidents,
- having a memory that just keeps coming back,
- hearing jokes about sexual abuse,
- being criticized or feeling attacked for something you said or did,
- hearing or seeing something that reminds you of the abuse,
- having nightmares or daydreams about the abuse,
- being touched by others, even in a nonsexual way,
- feeling trapped, or
- seeing a color or pattern in your environment.

Even something unrelated to your sexual abuse can become a trigger. For example, you might find yourself getting anxious about an upcoming test, performance, game, or meeting—way more anxious than you used to get. Just the intense anxious feeling itself can activate your brain and body and be triggering.

Flashbacks

Flashbacks occur when you re-experience memories so vividly or intensely that they actually feel real.[3] If you have flashbacks related to your sexual abuse, it can feel as if it is happening all over again. It is important to know that you don't cause triggering or flashbacks. They just happen. Even though you don't cause them, you might still judge yourself harshly for having them. But before you do that, go back and look at the circumstances. Try to make connections and figure out what happened and how you got triggered. Look at the list above to help you discover what caused it. In time, you will get good at figuring out what may be triggering for you and take extra care when these situations arise.

You may not be able to stop your flashbacks right now, but it is good to know what causes them and how to take care of yourself when they happen. Once you become aware that you are triggered or having a flashback, the best thing you can do is immediately use your calming skills. Do some breath work (Chapter 14), a Body Check (Chapter 15), or use one of your other Big Skills (Chapter 16). If needed, repeat them until the intensity passes, and you become calm and feel Just Right again.

It's Time to Get Help

Flashbacks are re-traumatizing. They are also a sign that you may have PTSD.[4] If you have flashbacks about your sexual abuse, you will need to get help from a trauma-trained therapist. They have specialized training in trauma healing therapies designed to resolve these types of traumatic memories. Don't delay. Flashbacks will not go away on their own.[5] If left untreated, some people have flashbacks for decades. There is no reason to suffer needlessly and endlessly. You will need professional assistance with this.

The intensity and frequency of flashbacks will lessen as you work on them with your trauma-trained therapist. The traumatic memories will get re-processed out of the primitive part of your brain and get stored right along with all of your other non-traumatic memories.[6] They will become just "normal" memories.[7] Sad ones, to be sure, but not traumatic ones anymore. Most importantly, they will no longer have the power to overwhelm you.[8] Further, people who work through their traumatic memories in this way often report a profound sense of relief as these memories find their proper place.

What's true for you?

Do you have flashbacks? If so, think about a recent one. Use the list in this chapter to help identify what triggered you.

If you did not use your calming skills at the time, re-imagine that same flashback. This time, in your mind's eye, see yourself remembering to use a skill and calming back down.

If you haven't done so already, what steps can you take now to begin working with a trauma-trained therapist in order to resolve your flashbacks?

21

NIGHTMARES

GETTING a good night's sleep most nights is crucial to your overall functioning and mental health,[1] but in the aftermath of sexual abuse, your normal sleep patterns can be affected.[2] If you practice good sleep hygiene[3] and use the calming skills learned in Chapter 14 (Breath Work), Chapter 15 (Body Checks), and Chapter 16 (More Big Skills), you should be able to get a good night's sleep on a regular basis. However, even with the best intentions and preparation, your sleep can still be disturbed by nightmares. Sometimes, the same nightmare or some version of it is repeated over and over. In this chapter, you will learn how to deal directly with nightmares since they can be common in the aftermath of sexual abuse.[4]

If you have nightmares, there can be a tendency to want to avoid going to sleep or try drugs or alcohol to "zone out." This can lead to

85

substance abuse, addictions, and depression, so be very careful. Also, alcohol and drugs only sedate, which is very different from natural restorative sleep.[5] They may temporarily numb you to the fact that it is hard to get calm and relaxed right now, but they don't fix anything. After the sedation wears off, your problems are still there. So, it is best to deal with your nightmares directly if they are preventing you from sleeping well most nights.

The approach to working with nightmares described below is adapted from Dr. Stephen Aizenstat's book *Dream Tending*.[6] He is an expert in dreamwork and has worked all over the world with all sorts of people and all sorts of nightmares.

How to Work with Nightmares

Put pen and paper or a journal by your bed so you can write down your dreams upon waking. Write down whatever you can remember, even if it is just a snippet or a feeling. Work with nightmares when you are fully awake and have a little distance from the dream but can still recall what happened. Courage and a little preparation are required to work with nightmares. There are six steps.

Step 1: Get Calm

Take a couple of minutes and get calm by doing Three Breaths or Seven Belly Breaths (Chapter 14) and a Body Check (Chapter 15).

Step 2: Bring Help

Next, arm yourself with some *imaginal* help. Don't approach your nightmare alone. Have an imaginal friend (or friends) stand with you. You might be able to find some support from inside the dream itself, so go back inside the dreamscape and look around. What else do you see? You may notice other things you missed when you were focused on the scariest part(s). You may discover another person or animal present in the dream that you had not noticed before. If friendly, invite that other figure to help you.

If you do not find a helpful figure from inside the dream or do not want to go looking there for one, you can always get support from outside the dream. In this case, imagine yourself accompanied by a trusted ally or allies. They can be real people or an animal in your life that you trust. They can also be historical, mythical, or imaginal figures. (Even Harry Potter had Ron, Hermione, Dumbledore, and Hagrid!) Who do you want with you as you do this work?

Step 3: Stand Your Ground

In your mind, return to the dreamscape again, only this time bring your imaginal ally or allies with you. Go toward the scary dream figure. If a wave of fear comes over you, notice it, and see if you can let it pass. Breathe. Notice how big or powerful the figure is compared to you and your allies. Let some time go by and notice how you feel standing up to the figure. Stand your ground. Now, get face to face and toe to toe with it.

Caution: *If you become overwhelmed, stop and use your calming skills. Do Seven Belly Breaths and a Body Check. Get completely calm again before resuming the exercise.*

If you feel good enough, then keep going. Stand up tall. Feel yourself becoming strong and confident with your ally (or allies) by your side. Let the figure know that you can stand up for yourself now and that you will fight back if necessary. Talk to it in a clear and direct way. Let the figure know that you are not afraid and that you will not be moved. Express yourself long enough and with enough force that the figure backs off.

Step 4: Get Curious

Once it backs off, get curious about the dream figure. You can look at the figure more closely now since you are no longer running away or terrified. Observe it and watch what it says or does. Ask the figure, "Why are you in my dreams," and "Why are you here now?"

Write down whatever the figure says. Notice any sound(s) that it makes. Look away and imitate the sound. Repeat it as loudly as you can. Let the figure know that you are powerful and able to fight. Get as much information from and about the figure as possible. How does this figure try to control you? Does it remind you of someone else in your life? What are they trying to take from you?

Step 5: Reclaim Your Power

Now, it is time to reclaim your power. Order the figure to stay back and to leave you alone! Tell it that you are not afraid of it anymore and to quit bothering you. Finally, in your fiercest voice and with all your determination, command it to "GO AWAY!" Find whatever words work best for you. Repeat them firmly and over and over until the figure finally backs off. Then you will have some breathing room and some safety.

It is not easy to work with nightmares, but you will get to this point if you can hang in there and follow the steps. Either the nightmares will end and the frightening figure(s) will stop showing up in your dreams, or they will not come nearly as often or be as intense. Also, you will have learned how to face something that has been terrifying you.

Step 6: Stop the Cycle

Your traumatic fight/flight or freeze response can be activated during or after nightmares, so you may need to take some time and calm yourself and your system back down again. Sometimes, getting out of bed or telling someone about the dream isn't enough. To shake it off and get back to feeling Just Right, you may need to get your body moving and do something physical. Try doing sit-ups or push-ups, going for a walk, or taking a shower. Sometimes, depending upon the nightmare's intensity, it may take a few hours to calm down again completely.

Finally, if you don't have nightmares, you may be disturbed by "Too Cool-type dreams" that feel hazy or cloudy with haunting dream figures that are barely identifiable. When you feel ready, you can invite those dream figures to come out of the shadows, quit hiding, and come closer. As you do so, work with the figure(s) using the six steps listed above.

The importance of routinely getting a good night's sleep for your mental health cannot be overemphasized. If you are disturbed by nightmares, follow the steps in this chapter and deal with them. This is an important aspect of tending the wound of your sexual abuse. It will empower you, help ease your mind, and allow you to get the benefits of a good night's sleep most nights.

What's true for you?

Has your sleep been affected because of your sexual abuse? If so, how? What can you do to get yourself back into a good sleep routine?

If you have nightmares, work with one that is fresh in your mind using the steps in this chapter.

VI

THE WAY AHEAD

22

STAYING SAFE NOW

IN reaching this point in the guide, you have had to look honestly at yourself and have done some challenging psychological work—perhaps some of the hardest you may ever do. You have educated yourself about the wound of sexual abuse, and by now, you should be starting to take care of yourself and properly tend your wound. Hopefully, you are also getting the kinds of support you need right now as well. In this last section of the guide, you will learn what to expect in the months and years ahead. This chapter provides timely information on how to keep yourself safe going forward.

After experiencing sexual abuse, many people find that they are vulnerable to being hurt again and need to be protective of themselves for a while.[1] Studies show that in the aftermath of sexual abuse, there is a higher risk for

- being sexually abused again,
- developing anxiety, depression, or PTSD,
- attempting or completing suicide,
- having unsafe sex,
- alcohol abuse,
- drug abuse,
- becoming a sexual abuser later in life, and
- if you are younger, teen pregnancy.[2]

This is a fragile time, and the list above is a reminder to remain aware. Right now, you may have to work a little harder day in and day out to keep yourself safe. You will have to pay closer attention to those around you and remain aware when unwanted people approach you.

Some people even have an uncanny feeling of somehow being "marked" at first, as if others are somehow drawn to them to abuse or exploit them all over again. This is because the wound is open and raw, and predators have a way of trying to latch on to those who are vulnerable. Also, some people find themselves unconsciously winding up in dangerous or compromising situations over and over again.[3]

If you become aware that any of these things are happening, it may be necessary for you to overcorrect for a while to keep yourself safe as you work through your trauma. In doing so, you will become stronger and wisely protective—not only of yourself but of others. For a period of time, this may mean opting out of some things that create a greater risk for you and choosing to avoid situations where certain people or activities will be present. You can choose to stop any "unhealthy coping behaviors" and work on your issues directly.

Despite your best efforts, if you still feel out of control or can't keep yourself safe, then at least start thinking about what you are doing *while* you are in these situations. Lean in and get closer to your experience of what is actually going on for you in real time while these things are happening. Stopping and thinking about what is really going on while it is happening is a powerful technique. It is a way of waking yourself up to the truth, and it will help you make connections between your past abuse and what is going on for you in the moment.

Taking care of yourself and staying safe may cause you to feel a little isolated and alone at times, but you are not going through this by yourself. In the United States, it is estimated that one in four girls and one in thirteen boys experience sexual abuse in childhood.[4] For adults, one in five women and one in forty men experience rape, and nearly one in two women and one in four men experience sexual violence other than rape in their lifetimes.[5] So, as you begin to look around and get connected, you may find others who have been suffering in silence. School clubs, community organizations, and therapists may be able to assist in connecting you with others trying to tend their wounds. Having a community of support is healing.[6]

What's true for you?

Do you find yourself doing dangerous things or ending up in unsafe situations? These may be signs that you haven't fully learned how to tend the wound of sexual abuse yet. What can you do to make things safer for yourself?

23

TRAUMA ANNIVERSARIES

WHETHER you want it to or not, your mind keeps its own unconscious calendar, and it has a way of remembering the anniversaries of really tough times. No matter how much healing and time goes by, the anniversary or anniversaries of your sexual abuse may have some effect on you.[1] This does not mean that all your hard work was in vain. It just means that your body and your deep mind remember what happened. Don't forget that sexual abuse is a special kind of wound. Periodically, it may still require some tending—even when you are much older.

If your abuse occurred around a major holiday or at a particular time of year, you might notice yourself struggling during those times. Each anniversary is different. Some pass easily and without notice. With others, you may struggle a little or even find yourself having a really difficult time. These are signs that your wound is reacting to the anniversary of your trauma. It remembers. Just be aware that you may be a little more tender or raw during those times of the year.

You might also find that other significant life events like having children, getting married, or deaths may be more complicated for you in some ways. You might find yourself struggling during pregnancy or when your child approaches the age at which your abuse occurred. Even if you don't have distinct memories of your abuse, you might just notice yourself feeling depressed or agitated. It can be that subtle.

Slow down and be very gentle with yourself if you struggle during an anniversary. It is also good to share what you are experiencing with others who love you. Just talking about it and feeling supported can be very beneficial during these times.

If a trauma anniversary or life event gets too intense, find a trauma-trained therapist, and do some more work around your abuse. In no way does this mean you are failing in your efforts. It is actually a sign that authentic healing is ongoing and that some aspect of your wound needs a little extra attention. That part of your wound simply was not ready to be dealt with way back when you were younger.

What's true for you?
What time(s) of the year might cause your wound to ache again? How can you take care of yourself during your trauma anniversaries?

What significant future life events will require some extra self-care on your part? How do you plan to take care of yourself during those times?

24

BAD DAYS HAPPEN

TRAUMA anniversaries aside, it is important to remember that you will always have some bad days regardless of how well you tend the wound of your sexual abuse. Sometimes you can see them coming and can brace yourself, and then there are other times when you just feel really off or overwhelmed all over again for no apparent reason. Bad days are a normal part of life for everyone. In your case, they may be more closely tied to your sexual abuse.

What can you do when bad days happen? Having worked your way through this guide, you can probably guess the answer to this question. The best thing you can do is . . . let them come. Go toward the down feelings. Take some extra time to care for yourself. Let those who love you know that you are having a hard day. Go to bed early or sleep in if you can. Take an extra-long bath. Slow down. Take a walk.

Journal. Go easy on yourself. Give yourself permission to just go ahead and have a hard day (or two or three).

Be careful not to get down on yourself for feeling bad. Sometimes, you may even feel like wanting to give up or believe that nothing has changed. But don't believe those old lies. (It's funny how they always come around just when you are feeling at your worst!)

The truth is that all your hard work does matter, and it does count. You matter, and you count. It is always good to remind yourself that healing is not linear. *It's circular.* On bad days, you are just coming back around again to all the hard stuff.[1] Your job is to tend the wound, try and tolerate it, go easy on yourself, and give it some time to pass.

What's true for you?
Are you able to go easy on yourself when you are having a bad day or a rough week? What are some things you can do or tell yourself next time you go through a tough time that will make it easier to bear?

CONCLUSION

THIS guide has introduced you to some difficult truths about the wounding caused by sexual abuse. In Chapter 2, sexual abuse was described as a special kind of wound that requires special care. Even with all the good work you have done so far, it will still need some care at various times throughout life. Accepting these first big difficult truths is good preparation for whatever else comes your way. You will discover other truths for yourself as you go along.

An old African proverb says, "The wound carries the medicine." In this case, your medicine is found in the wound of your sexual abuse—the very thing you may have been trying to avoid when you first picked up this guide. Avoidance only adds to suffering and can cause you to act out (or act in) in all sorts of ways. If you don't learn how to tend it, this type of wound can fester and become the source of much misery in your life. Respect its power to harm or to heal. Teach yourself to tend it properly. The best way to deal with your sexual abuse is not only to accept it but to remember it, stay close to it, and work through it.[1]

Over and over, throughout this guide, you have been asked to lean in and go toward hard feelings, emotions, memories, bodily sensations, and nightmares and not to avoid them or push them away. Mythologist and comparative religion scholar Joseph Campbell said, "The cave you fear to enter holds the treasure you seek." The only way out of this is through it. Going toward frightening things requires tremendous courage. Don't go it alone. Get the support you need and deserve by relying on the team you put together for yourself back in Chapter 7. You stand with all others who have suffered in their own unique ways. In doing this work, you have learned to tend a deep wound. And, if you so choose, you can also be there for others.

Finally, return to this guide throughout your life whenever the wound starts aching again. Authentic healing is a slow work. Practice the basic calming skills over and over into old age. It is a life's work and well worth it. You owe it to yourself now, and you owe it to your future self.

What's true for you?

Congratulations! You have read this guide and allowed yourself to think about some really hard things. You have done some very difficult psychological work. This is not an easy thing to do for anyone—at any age. Pause for a moment and claim this accomplishment for yourself.

Imagine times throughout your life when your mind will naturally circle back to your sexual abuse. Hold yourself in your mind's eye with love and gentleness. Write a supportive letter telling yourself what you would most want to hear at those times.

Appendix A
Online Resources

Psychology Today. (https://www.psychologytoday.com)
Enter a ZIP Code or city to get a list of therapists near you.

RAINN. (https://www.rainn.org)
Education and research on sexual assault. Hotline and chat line.

Local Domestic Violence Shelter. (https://www.domesticshelters.org)
Enter ZIP Code or city and get a list of local resources.

Local Anti-Violence Project. (https://avp.org)
Supports LGBTQ survivors. There are local chapters and a hotline.

Know Your IX. (https://www.knowyourix.org)
Survivor and Youth-led. Trying to end sexual violence in schools.

End Rape on Campus. (http://endrapeoncampus.org)
Working to end rape on college campuses.

The Consensual Project. (http://www.theconsensualproject.com)
Partners with schools to educate on consent.

National Sexual Violence Resource Center. (https://www.nsvrc.org)
Resources for survivors.

National Alliance to End Sexual Assault.
(http://www.endsexualviolence.org)
Focuses on legislation to support survivors and prevention.

NO MORE. (https://nomore.org)
Coalition for the prevention of sexual violence.

APPENDIX B
SEXUALLY ABUSED FAMOUS PEOPLE

The following is a brief list of famous people who were sexually abused as children or teens.

Maya Angelou	Oprah Winfrey
Mo'Nique	Carlos Santana
Marilyn Monroe	Roseanne Barr
Tim Roth	Antone Fisher
Queen Latifah	Fiona Apple
McKayla Maroney	Derek Luke
Missy Elliot	Rosie Perez
Jane Fonda	Madonna
Billie Holiday	Mary J. Blige
Anthony Edwards	Ashley Judd
Minnie Driver	Jade Roper
Corey Haim	Gabrielle Union
Lady Gaga	Common
Fantasia	Axl Rose
Ellen DeGeneres	Sally Field
Padma Lakshmi	Johannes Brahms
Vanessa Williams	Teri Hatcher
Corey Feldman	Tyler Perry
Anne Heche	Anna Lynne McCord
Cheryl Burke	Henry Rollins
Margaret Cho	America Ferrera
Jaime King	Drew Barrymore

Sources:
https://www.ranker.com/list/famous-survivors-of-child-abuse/celebrity-lists
https://www.ranker.com/list/celebrities-who-were-sexually-abused/celebrity-lists
https://www.sheknows.com/entertainment/slideshow/5839/celebs-whove-spoken-out-about-being-sexually-assaulted/1/
https://www.marieclaire.com/celebrity/news/g3478/celebrities-victims-sexual-assault/

Appendix C
Why Keep Trying

When I am struggling and things are difficult for me, these are the reasons why I want to keep trying:

1.

2.

3.

4.

5.

6.

7.

cut and post

APPENDIX D
BREATH WORK AND BODY CHECKS

Cut out the instructions below and keep them in your wallet. Also, take a picture and store them in your phone.

Seven Belly Breaths
1. One hand on chest. Other hand on belly.
2. Find your breath.
3. If comfortable, close mouth. Exhale completely through the nose.
4. Inhale into belly and count, "One, one, one..."
5. Exhale fully still counting, "One, one, one ..."
6. Look for pause at end of exhale.
7. Repeat for 7 breaths, counting the whole time.
8. To end: One deep breath in and out. Notice.
9. Repeat, if needed. Start again with ones.

Three Breaths

Stop what you are doing. Pay attention. Take three breaths.

Body Checks
1. Wiggle your toes. Notice what your feet or heels are touching.
2. Tense and hold legs for 5 seconds. Relax. Repeat 3 times.
3. Notice your buttocks as you shift your weight side to side.
4. Notice where back touches and where it does not.
5. Move head around like when stretching your neck. Relax your jaw. Notice.
6. Make fists and tense arms for 5 seconds. Relax. Repeat 3 times.
7. Rub one finger with thumb. Notice how finger feels.
8. Now rub thumb with that finger. Notice how your thumb feels.
9. Do other hand.
10. Notice how you feel now. Repeat if needed.

Appendix E
Imaginal Dialogues

Work with strong feelings and emotions, inner figures, or numbness by engaging with them in an imaginal dialogue. List what or who you want to work with in the space below:

_____

Now, write down your responses to the following prompts on a piece of paper.

- When thinking about this inner voice or figure, feeling, or emotion, what image comes to mind? Draw the image. Write a description of it with as much detail as you can. Get specific. This is your image of it. Today. Right now. Pause in your mind and ask these questions: What does it look like? Is it animate or inanimate? Does it have a shape? Is it hard or soft? Does it have edges? What color is it? Is it big or small? Young or old? Does it have a name? And so on.
- Describe what it feels like to you.
- Where is it in your body? Put your hands on those parts. What happens if you breathe into those parts?
- Describe how it sounds.
- Now, speak with the image. Ask it to talk. Let it say what it wants to say. Write down whatever it says.
- Respond to what the image said. Write down your response.
- Don't banish the image, and don't run away from it. Stay curious if you can. Continuing talking with it. Ask it, "Why are you here now," and "What do you want to say?" Listen for the responses and write down what it says.

- Keep the conversation going back and forth. Write down what each of you says. Keep asking it questions. Tell the image what you want it to know. Listen to its responses.
- Write down your imaginal dialogue as it unfolds.

You can also engage with the image in other ways. For example, make a movement or get into a position that shows what this image feels like to you. Then make a movement or position your body in response. Continue moving, back and forth, just as in the conversation.

Pay attention to what happens with the emotion, feeling, or inner figure. It may morph from one thing into another. Your relationship with it may change. Whatever happens, let it shift and evolve. Write down or draw any changes. Notice any shifts in how you feel or think as you do this work.

NOTES

PREFACE

1. Kerr, "Window of Tolerance Guide."

INTRODUCTION

1. For additional resources, see Brohl and Potter, *When Your Child Has Been Molested;* and Davis, *Allies in Healing: When the Person You Love Was Sexually Abused as a Child.*

2. See Ferenczi, "Confusion of Tongues between Adults and the Child"; Freud, "Remembering, Repeating and Working-through"; Jung, "A Review of the Complex Theory"; Jung, "On the Nature of the Psyche"; Peláez, "Trauma Theory in Sándor Ferenczi's Writings of 1931 and 1932;" Van der Hart, Brown, and Van der Kolk, "Janet's Treatment of Post-Traumatic Stress."

3. See Bass and Davis, *Beginning to Heal;* Herman, *Trauma and Recovery;* Levine, *Waking the Tiger;* Levine and Kline, *Trauma through a Child's Eyes;* Van der Kolk, *The Body Keeps the Score.*

4. For examples of the hero's journey motif, see Campbell, *The Hero with a Thousand Faces;* Heiko, *A Therapist's Guide to Mapping the Girl Heroine's Journey in Sandplay;* Murdock, *The Heroine's Journey;* and Scruggs, *There's a Secret in the Village.*

CHAPTER 1— SEXUAL ABUSE AND TREATMENT

1. American Psychological Association, "Sexual Abuse."

2. United States Department of Justice, "Sexual Assault."

3. United States Department of Justice, "An Updated Definition of Rape."

4. World Health Organization Social Change and Mental Health Violence and Injury Prevention, "Report of the Consultation on Child Abuse Prevention," 15–16.

5. Murray, Nguyen, and Cohen, "Child Sexual Abuse," 322.

6. Leeb et al., "Child Maltreatment Surveillance: Uniform Definitions for Public Health and Recommended Data Elements (Version 1.0)," 14–15.

7. Murray, Nguyen, and Cohen, "Child Sexual Abuse" 322; Also see Finkelhor, "What's Wrong with Sex between Adults and Children?" for an ethical argument against sex between adults and minors and the rationale for why minors are incapable of giving full and informed consent.

8. Brown and Finkelhor, "Impact of Child Sexual Abuse. A Review of the Research," 74–76.

9. Dube et al., "Long-Term Consequences of Childhood Sexual Abuse by Gender of Victim," 436.

10. Irish, Kobayashi, and Delahanty, "Long-Term Physical Health Consequences of Childhood Sexual Abuse," 457–58.

11. Kilpatrick, Saunders, and Smith, "Youth Victimization: Prevalence and Implications," ii.

12. Trask, Walsh, and DiLillo, "Treatment Effects for Common Outcomes of Child Sexual Abuse," 6.

13. Shapiro, *Eye Movement Desensitization and Reprocessing (EMDR)*.

14. Monson, *Treating PTSD with Cognitive–Behavioral Therapies*.

15. Chertoff, "Psychodynamic Assessment and Treatment of Traumatized Patients," 46.

16. Resick and Schnicke, *Cognitive Processing Therapy for Rape Victims*.

17. Rosenzweig, "Some Implicit Common Factors in Diverse Methods of Psychotherapy," 414–15; Shapiro and Shapiro, "Meta-Analysis of Comparative Therapy Outcome Studies," 581.

CHAPTER 2—A SPECIAL KIND OF WOUND

1. Jung, "A Review of the Complex Theory," 103.

2. Balint, "*The Basic Fault*," 183; and Jung, "The Psychological Foundations of Belief in Spirits, 1948," 313–14.

3. Siegel, *Mindsight*, 160–61.

4. Herman, *Trauma and Recovery*, 1; Levine and Kline, *Trauma through a Child's Eyes*, 262; Spröber et al., "Child Sexual Abuse in Religiously Affiliated and Secular Institutions," 1.

5. Brown and Finkelhor, "Impact of Child Sexual Abuse. A Review of the Research," 66.

6. See Levine, *Trauma and Memory*, xix-xxii; Ogden, Minton, and Pain, *Trauma and the Body*, 3-25; and Van der Kolk, *The Body Keeps the Score*, 74-76.

7. Brewin, *Posttraumatic Stress Disorder*, 56–57.

8. Stolorow, *Trauma and Human Existence*, 16.

9. Barth et al., "The Current Prevalence of Child Sexual Abuse Worldwide," 469-70; Centers for Disease Control and Prevention, "Preventing Child Sexual

Abuse"; Singh, Parsekar, and Nair, "An Epidemiological Overview of Child Sexual Abuse," 430-33.

CHAPTER 3—DIFFICULT MEMORIES

1. See Levine, *Trauma and Memory*, xix-xxii; Ogden, Minton, and Pain, *Trauma and the Body*, 3-25; and Van der Kolk, *The Body Keeps the Score*, 74-76.
2. Herman, *Trauma and Recovery*, 37–42.

CHAPTER 4—MAKING SENSE

1. Bass and Davis, *Beginning to Heal*, 120–28.
2. Steele, van der Hart, and Nijenhuis, "Phase-Oriented Treatment of Structural Dissociation in Complex Traumatization," 37.
3. Kalsched, *The Inner World of Trauma*, 95.
4. Bass and Davis, *Beginning to Heal*, 120–28.
5. Siegel, *The Developing Mind*, 247–50.
6. Brewin, *Posttraumatic Stress Disorder*, 63–87.
7. Kalsched, *The Inner World of Trauma*, 24.
8. Herman, *Trauma and Recovery*, 51–56.
9. Finkelhor and Brown, "The Traumatic Impact of Child Sexual Abuse: A Conceptualization," 536.

CHAPTER 6—SUICIDAL THINKING

1. Dube et al., "Long-Term Consequences of Childhood Sexual Abuse by Gender of Victim," 433.
2. Briere, Madni, and Godbout, "Recent Suicidality in the General Population," 3064.
3. Hillman, *Suicide and the Soul*, 88.

CHAPTER 7—YOUR SUPPORT TEAM

1. Brewin, *Posttraumatic Stress Disorder*, 56–57.
2. Shapiro, *Eye Movement Desensitization and Reprocessing (EMDR)*, 125–27.
3. Winnicott, *Playing and Reality*, 8.
4. DeSalvo, *Writing as a Way of Healing*, 17–28.

CHAPTER 8— TRAINING YOUR BRAIN

1. Gazzaniga, *The Mind's Past*, 21.
2. Jung, "On the Nature of the Psyche," 186.
3. Miller, *Thou Shalt Not Be Aware*, 318.

CHAPTER 9—WHAT'S GOING ON INSIDE?

1. Ogden, Minton, and Pain, *Trauma and the Body*, 156.
2. Ogden, Minton, and Pain, 156.
3. Van der Kolk, *The Body Keeps the Score*, 51–58.
4. Briere and Elliott, "Immediate and Long-Term Impacts of Child Sexual Abuse," 56–62.
5. Levine and Kline, *Trauma through a Child's Eyes*, 66–71.

6. Herman, *Trauma and Recovery*, 51–56.
7. Van der Kolk, *The Body Keeps the Score*, 51–102.
8. Van der Kolk, 66–69.

CHAPTER 10—TOO HOT

1. Levine, *Waking the Tiger*, 132–34.
2. Levine and Kline, *Trauma through a Child's Eyes*, 4–8.
3. Bourne, Mackay, and Holmes, "The Neural Basis of Flashback Formation," 1528–29.

CHAPTER 11—TOO COLD

1. Levine, *Waking the Tiger*, 132–44.
2. Levine, 99–108.
3. Levine, 132–44.
4. Van der Kolk, *The Body Keeps the Score*, 66–67.
5. Van der Kolk, 66–67.

CHAPTER 12— GETTING JUST RIGHT

1. Zoja, *Where Soul Meets Matter*, 15.
2. Ogden, Minton, and Pain, *Trauma and the Body*, 26–40.
3. Kalsched, *The Inner World of Trauma*, 97.

CHAPTER 13—LEAN IN TO DISCOMFORT

1. Ogden, Minton, and Pain, *Trauma and the Body*, 26.
2. Seif and Winston, *What Every Therapist Needs to Know about Anxiety Disorders*, 37–52.
3. Jung, "A Review of the Complex Theory," 99.
4. Seif and Winston, *What Every Therapist Needs to Know about Anxiety Disorders*, 37–52, 70–83.
5. Jung, "On the Nature of the Psyche," 187.

CHAPTER 14—BREATHE

1. See Rama, Ballentine, and Hymes, *Science of Breath*; and Rosen, *The Yoga of Breath*.
2. Van der Kolk, *The Body Keeps the Score*, 268–69.
3. Gunaratana, *Mindfulness in Plain English*, 53–55.
4. Gunaratana, 53–55, 116–17.
5. Bernhard, *How to Be Sick*, 128-29.

CHAPTER 15—BODY CHECKS

1. Levine, *In an Unspoken Voice*, 76.
2. Emerson and Hopper, *Overcoming Trauma through Yoga*, 111–12.

CHAPTER 16—MORE BIG SKILLS

1. Van der Kolk, *The Body Keeps the Score*, 242–43.
2. DeSalvo, *Writing as a Way of Healing*, 25–28.

3. Van der Kolk, *The Body Keeps the Score*, 242–43.
4. Van der Kolk, 271–76.
5. Van der Kolk, 274.
6. Boyd, Lanius, and McKinnon, "Mindfulness-Based Treatments for Posttraumatic Stress Disorder," 22.
7. See Kabat-Zinn, *Mindfulness for Beginners*; and Gunaratana, *Mindfulness in Plain English*.

CHAPTER 17—STRONG EMOTIONS AND INNER CRITICS

1. Jung and Chodorow, *Jung on Active Imagination*, 53–60.
2. Johnson, Inner Work, 137-42; Von Franz, *Psychotherapy*, 163-76.
3. Von Franz, *Psychotherapy*, 163-76.

CHAPTER 18—NUMBNESS

1. Siegel, *Mindsight*, 157–58.
2. Ogden, Minton, and Pain, *Trauma and the Body*, 133–34.
3. Jung and Chodorow, *Jung on Active Imagination*, 53–62.

CHAPTER 19—"BIG T" TRAUMA

1. Shapiro, *Eye Movement Desensitization and Reprocessing (EMDR)*, 4–5.
2. American Psychiatric Association, *Diagnostic and Statistical Manual of Mental Disorders*, 271–80.

CHAPTER 20—TRIGGERS AND FLASHBACKS

1. American Psychiatric Association, *Diagnostic and Statistical Manual of Mental Disorders*, 271.
2. Van der Kolk, *The Body Keeps the Score*, 66–70.
3. Siegel, *Mindsight*, 145–89.
4. American Psychiatric Association, *Diagnostic and Statistical Manual of Mental Disorders*, 271.
5. Siegel, *Mindsight*, 163.
6. Shapiro, *Eye Movement Desensitization and Reprocessing (EMDR)*, 29–34.
7. Van der Kolk, *The Body Keeps the Score*, 175–76.
8. Jung, "On the Nature of the Psyche," 186–87.

CHAPTER 21—NIGHTMARES

1. Walker, *Why We Sleep*, 107–32.
2. Steine et al., "Sleep Disturbances in Sexual Abuse Victims," 15.
3. For a list of tips on a healthy sleep routine, see Walker, *Why We Sleep*, 341–42.
4. Siegel, *Mindsight*, 158–59.
5. Walker, *Why We Sleep*, 282–92.
6. Aizenstat, *Dream Tending*, 61–88.

CHAPTER 22—STAYING SAFE NOW

1. Freud, "Remembering, Repeating and Working-through," 151.
2. Putnam, "Ten-Year Research Update Review," 271–73.

3. Freud, "Remembering, Repeating and Working-through," 151.

4. Centers for Disease Control and Prevention, "Preventing Child Sexual Abuse."

5. Smith et al., "The National Intimate Partner and Sexual Violence Survey: 2015 Data Brief — Updated Release," 2–3.

6. Herman, *Trauma and Recovery*, 73.

CHAPTER 23—TRAUMA ANNIVERSARIES

1. Mintz, "The Anniversary Reaction" 720; Dlin and Keith Fischer, "The Anniversary Reaction," 753.

CHAPTER 24—BAD DAYS HAPPEN

1. Jung, "A Review of the Complex Theory," 93.

CONCLUSION

1. Balint, "*The Basic Fault*," 183; and Freud, "Remembering, Repeating and Working-through," 154–55.

BIBLIOGRAPHY

Aizenstat, Stephen. *Dream Tending*. New Orleans: Spring Journal, 2009.

American Psychiatric Association. *Diagnostic and Statistical Manual of Mental Disorders: DSM-5*. 5th ed. Arlington, VA: American Psychiatric Association, 2013.

American Psychological Association. "Sexual Abuse." Psychology Topics. Accessed November 14, 2020. https://www.apa.org/topics/sexual-abuse.

Balint, Michael. *The Basic Fault: Therapeutic Aspects of Regression*. New York: Bruner/Mazel, Publishers, 1968.

Barth, J., L. Bermetz, E. Heim, S. Trelle, and T. Tonia. "The Current Prevalence of Child Sexual Abuse Worldwide: A Systematic Review and Meta-Analysis." *International Journal of Public Health* 58, no. 3 (2013): 469–83. https://doi.org/10.1007/s00038-012-0426-1.

Bass, Ellen, and Laura Davis. *Beginning to Heal: A First Book for Survivors of Child Sexual Abuse*. New York: HarperCollins, 1993.

Bernhard, Toni. *How to Be Sick: A Buddhist-Inspired Guide for the Chronically Ill and Their Caregivers*. Somerville, MA: Wisdom Publications, 2018.

Bourne, C., C. E. Mackay, and E. A. Holmes. "The Neural Basis of Flashback Formation: The Impact of Viewing Trauma." *Psychological Medicine* 43, no. 7 (2013): 1521–32. https://doi.org/10.1017/S0033291712002358.

Boyd, Jenna E., Ruth A. Lanius, and Margaret C. McKinnon. "Mindfulness-Based Treatments for Posttraumatic Stress Disorder: A Review of the Treatment Literature and Neurobiological Evidence." *Journal of Psychiatry & Neuroscience* 43, no. 1 (2018): 7–25. https://doi.org/10.1503/jpn.170021.

Brewin, Chris. *Post-Traumatic Stress Disorder: Malady or Myth?* New Haven, CT: Yale University Press, 2003.

Briere, John, Laila A. Madni, and Natacha Godbout. "Recent Suicidality in the General Population: Multivariate Association with Childhood Maltreatment and Adult Victimization." *Journal of Interpersonal Violence* 31, no. 18 (2016): 3063–79. https://doi.org/10.1177/0886260515584339.

Briere, John N., and Diana M. Elliott. "Immediate and Long-Term Impacts of Child Sexual Abuse." *The Future of Children* 4, no. 2 (1994): 54–69. https://doi.org/10.2307/1602523.

Brohl, Kathryn, and Joyce Case Potter. *When Your Child Has Been Molested: A Parents' Guide to Healing and Recovery.* Rev. ed. San Francisco: Jossey-Bass, 2004.

Brown, Angela, and David Finkelhor. "Impact of Child Sexual Abuse. A Review of the Research." *Psychological Bulletin* 99, no. 1 (1986): 66–77. https://doi.org/10.1037/0033-2909.99.1.66.

Campbell, Joseph. *The Hero with a Thousand Faces.* 2nd ed. Princeton, NJ: Princeton University Press, 1973.

Centers for Disease Control and Prevention. "Preventing Child Sexual Abuse." Child Abuse & Neglect. Accessed November 14, 2020. https://www.cdc.gov/violenceprevention/childabuseandneglect/childsexualab use.html.

Chertoff, Judith. "Psychodynamic Assessment and Treatment of Traumatized Patients." *The Journal of Psychotherapy Practice and Research* 7, no. 1 (1998): 35–46. https://www.ncbi.nlm.nih.gov/pmc/articles/PMC3330481/.

Davis, Laura. *Allies in Healing: When the Person You Love Was Sexually Abused as a Child.* New York: William Morrow, 1991.

DeSalvo, Louise A. *Writing as a Way of Healing: How Telling Our Stories Transforms Our Lives.* Boston: Beacon, 2000.

Dlin, Barney M., and H. Keith Fischer. "The Anniversary Reaction: A Meeting of Freud and Pavlov." *Psychosomatics* 20, no. 11 (1979): 749–55. https://doi.org/10.1016/S0033-3182(79)73737-6.

Dube, Shanta R., Robert F. Anda, Charles L. Whitfield, David W. Brown, Vincent J. Felitti, Maxia Dong, and Wayne H. Giles. "Long-Term Consequences of Childhood Sexual Abuse by Gender of Victim." *American Journal of Preventive Medicine* 28, no. 5 (2005): 430–38. https://doi.org/10.1016/j.amepre.2005.01.015.

Emerson, David, and Elizabeth Hopper. *Overcoming Trauma through Yoga: Reclaiming Your Body.* Berkeley, CA: North Atlantic Books, 2011.

Ferenczi, Sandor. "Confusion of Tongues between Adults and the Child." In *Final Contributions to the Problems and Methods of Psychoanalysis (Vol. III)*, edited by Michael Balint, 156–67. New York: Basic Books, 1955.

Finkelhor, David. "What's Wrong with Sex between Adults and Children? Ethics and the Problem of Sexual Abuse." *American Journal of Orthopsychiatry* 49, no. 4 (1979): 692–97. https://doi.org/10.1111/j.1939-0025.1979.tb02654.x.

Finkelhor, David, and Angela Brown. "The Traumatic Impact of Child Sexual Abuse: A Conceptualization." *American Journal of Orthopsychiatry* 55, no. 4 (1985): 530–41.

Freud, Sigmund. "Remembering, Repeating and Working-through (Further Recommendations on the Technique of Psycho-Analysis II), 1914." In *The Standard Edition of the Complete Psychological Works of Sigmund Freud, Vol XII*, edited and translated by J. Strachey, 145–57. London: Hogarth Press, 1950.

Gazzaniga, Michael S. *The Mind's Past.* Berkeley, CA: University of California Press, 1998.

Gunaratana, Henepola. *Mindfulness in Plain English.* Boston: Wisdom Publications, 2002.

Heiko, Rosalind. *A Therapist's Guide to Mapping the Girl Heroine's Journey in Sandplay.* Lanham, MD: Rowman & Littlefield, 2018.

Herman, Judith. *Trauma and Recovery*. Rev. ed. New York: BasicBooks, 1997.

Hillman, James. *Suicide and the Soul*. Putnam, CT: Spring Publications, 2007.

Irish, Leah, Ihori Kobayashi, and Douglas L. Delahanty. "Long-Term Physical Health Consequences of Childhood Sexual Abuse: A Meta-Analytic Review." *Journal of Pediatric Psychology* 35, no. 5 (2010): 450–61. https://doi.org/10.1093/jpepsy/jsp118.

Johnson, Robert A. *Inner Work: Using Dreams & Active Imagination for Personal Growth*. New York: HarperOne, 1986.

Jung, C. G. "A Review of the Complex Theory" 1948. In *The Collected Works of C. G. Jung, Vol. 8: The Structure and Dynamics of the Psyche*, edited by Herbert Read, Michael Fordham, Gerhard Adler, and William McGuire, translated by R. F. C. Hull, 2nd ed., 92–105. Princeton, NJ: Princeton University Press, 1969.

———. "On the Nature of the Psyche," 1954. In *The Collected Works of C. G. Jung, Vol. 8: The Structure and Dynamics of the Psyche*, edited by Herbert Read, Michael Fordham, Gerhard Adler, and William McGuire, translated by R. F. C. Hull, 2nd ed., 159–234. Princeton, NJ: Princeton University Press, 1969.

———. "The Psychological Foundations of Belief in Spirits," 1948. In *The Collected Works of C. G. Jung, Vol. 8: The Structure and Dynamics of the Psyche*, edited by Herbert Read, Michael Fordham, Gerhard Adler, and William McGuire, translated by R. F. C. Hull, 2nd ed., 301–18. Princeton, NJ: Princeton University Press, 1969.

Jung, C. G., and Joan Chodorow. *Jung on Active Imagination*. Princeton, NJ: Princeton University Press, 1997.

Kabat-Zinn, Jon. *Mindfulness for Beginners: Reclaiming the Present Moment — and Your Life*. Boulder, CO: Sounds True, 2012.

Kalsched, Donald. *The Inner World of Trauma: Archetypal Defenses of the Personal Spirit*. London: Routledge, 1996.

Kerr, Laura K. "Window of Tolerance Guide." Laura K. Kerr, PhD - Writer and Scholar, 2008. https://www.laurakkerr.com/wot-guide/.

Kilpatrick, Dean G, Benjamin E Saunders, and Daniel W Smith. "Youth Victimization: Prevalence and Implications." U.S. Department of Justice, Office of Justice Programs, National Institute of Justice, 2003. https://www.ncjrs.gov/pdffiles1/nij/194972.pdf.

Leeb, Rebecca T., Leonard J. Paulozzi, Cindi Melanson, Thomas R. Simon, and Ileana Arias. "Child Maltreatment Surveillance: Uniform Definitions for Public Health and Recommended Data Elements (Version 1.0)." Centers for Disease Control and Prevention, 2008. http://www.cdc.gov/violenceprevention/pdf/cm_surveillance-a.pdf.

Levine, Peter A. *In an Unspoken Voice: How the Body Releases Trauma and Restores Goodness*. Berkeley, CA: North Atlantic Books, 2010.

———. *Trauma and Memory: Brain and Body in a Search for the Living Past*. Berkeley, CA: North Atlantic Books, 2015.

———. *Waking the Tiger: Healing Trauma*. Berkeley, CA: North Atlantic Books, 1997.

Levine, Peter A., and Maggie Kline. *Trauma through a Child's Eyes: Awakening the Ordinary Miracle of Healing*. Berkeley, CA: North Atlantic Books, 2006.

Miller, Alice. *Thou Shalt Not Be Aware: Society's Betrayal of the Child.* Translated by Hildegarde Hannum and Hunter Hannum. New York: Farrar, Straus and Giroux, 1984.

Mintz, Ira. "The Anniversary Reaction: A Response to the Unconscious Sense of Time." *Journal of the American Psychoanalytic Association* 19, no. 4 (1971): 720–35. https://doi.org/10.1177/000306517101900406.

Monson, Candice M. *Treating PTSD with Cognitive–Behavioral Therapies.* Washington, DC: American Psychological Association, 2014.

Murdock, Maureen. *The Heroine's Journey.* Boston: Shambhala, 1990.

Murray, Laura K., Amanda Nguyen, and Judith A. Cohen. "Child Sexual Abuse." *Child and Adolescent Psychiatric Clinics of North America* 23, no. 2 (2014): 321–37. https://doi.org/10.1016/j.chc.2014.01.003.

Ogden, Pat, Kekuni Minton, and Clare Pain. *Trauma and the Body: A Sensorimotor Approach to Psychotherapy.* New York: W.W. Norton, 2006.

Peláez, Miguel G. "Trauma Theory in Sándor Ferenczi's Writings of 1931 and 1932." *The International Journal of Psychoanalysis* 90, no. 6 (2009): 1217–33. https://doi.org/10.1111/j.1745-8315.2009.00190.x.

Putnam, Frank W. "Ten-Year Research Update Review: Child Sexual Abuse." *Journal of the American Academy of Child & Adolescent Psychiatry* 42, no. 3 (2003): 269–78. https://doi.org/10.1097/00004583-200303000-00006.

Rama, Swami, Rudolph Ballentine, and Alan Hymes. *Science of Breath: A Practical Guide.* Honesdale, PA: Himalayan Institute, 1998.

Resick, Patricia A., and Monica K. Schnicke. *Cognitive Processing Therapy for Rape Victims: A Treatment Manual.* Newbury Park, CA: SAGE, 1993.

Rosen, Richard. *The Yoga of Breath: A Step-by-Step Guide to Pranayama.* Boston: Shambhala, 2002.

Rosenzweig, Saul. "Some Implicit Common Factors in Diverse Methods of Psychotherapy." *American Journal of Orthopsychiatry* 6, no. 3 (1936): 412–15. https://doi.org/10.1111/j.1939-0025.1936.tb05248.x.

Scruggs, G. Kwame. *There's a Secret in the Village: Using Myth to Engage Urban Adolescent Males.* Saarbrücken, Germany: VDM Verlag Dr. Müller Aktiengesellschaft, 2010.

Seif, Martin N., and Sally Winston. *What Every Therapist Needs to Know about Anxiety Disorders: Key Concepts, Insights, and Interventions.* New York: Routledge, 2014.

Shapiro, David A., and Diana Shapiro. "Meta-Analysis of Comparative Therapy Outcome Studies: A Replication and Refinement." *Psychological Bulletin* 92, no. 3 (1982): 581–604. https://doi.org/10.1037/0033-2909.92.3.581.

Shapiro, Francine. *Eye Movement Desensitization and Reprocessing (EMDR): Basic Principles, Protocols, and Procedures.* 2nd ed. New York: Guilford, 2001.

Siegel, Daniel J. *Mindsight: The New Science of Personal Transformation.* New York: Bantam, 2010.

Singh, Mannat M., Shradha S. Parsekar, and Sreekumaran N. Nair. "An Epidemiological Overview of Child Sexual Abuse." *Journal of Family Medicine and Primary Care* 3, no. 4 (2014): 430–35. https://doi.org/10.4103/2249-4863.148139.

Smith, S. G., X. Zhang, K. C. Basile, M. T. Merrick, J. Wang, M. Kresnow, and J. Chen. "The National Intimate Partner and Sexual Violence Survey: 2015

Data Brief — Updated Release." Atlanta, GA: National Center for Injury Prevention and Control, Centers for Disease Control and Prevention, November 2018. https://www.cdc.gov/violenceprevention/pdf/2015data-brief508.pdf.

Spröber, Nina, Thekla Schneider, Miriam Rassenhofer, Alexander Seitz, Hubert Liebhardt, Lilith König, and Jörg M. Fegert. "Child Sexual Abuse in Religiously Affiliated and Secular Institutions: A Retrospective Descriptive Analysis of Data Provided by Victims in a Government-Sponsored Reappraisal Program in Germany." *BMC Public Health* 14, no. 1 (2014): 282: 1-12. https://doi.org/10.1186/1471-2458-14-282.

Steele, Kathy, Onno van der Hart, and Ellert R. S. Nijenhuis. "Phase-Oriented Treatment of Structural Dissociation in Complex Traumatization: Overcoming Trauma-Related Phobias." *Journal of Trauma & Dissociation* 6, no. 3 (2005): 11–53. https://doi.org/10.1300/J229v06n03_02.

Steine, Iris M., Allison G. Harvey, John H. Krystal, Anne M. Milde, Janne Grønli, Bjørn Bjorvatn, Inger H. Nordhus, Jarle Eid, and Ståle Pallesen. "Sleep Disturbances in Sexual Abuse Victims: A Systematic Review." *Sleep Medicine Reviews* 16, no. 1 (2012): 15–25. https://doi.org/10.1016/j.smrv.2011.01.006.

Stolorow, Robert D. *Trauma and Human Existence: Autobiographical, Psychoanalytic, and Philosophical Reflections.* New York: Analytic Press, 2007.

Trask, Emily V., Kate Walsh, and David DiLillo. "Treatment Effects for Common Outcomes of Child Sexual Abuse: A Current Meta-Analysis." *Aggression and Violent Behavior* 16, no. 1 (2011): 6–19. https://doi.org/10.1016/j.avb.2010.10.001.

United States Department of Justice. "An Updated Definition of Rape." U.S. Department of Justice Archives, Office of Public Affairs, January 6, 2012. https://www.justice.gov/archives/opa/blog/updated-definition-rape.

———. "Sexual Assault." U.S. Department of Justice, Office on Violence Against Women, May 16, 2019. https://www.justice.gov/ovw/sexual-assault.

Van der Hart, Onno, Paul Brown, and Bessel Van der Kolk. "Janet's Treatment of Post-Traumatic Stress." *Journal of Traumatic Stress* 2, no. 4 (1989): 379–95. https://doi.org/10.1007/BF00974597.

Van der Kolk, Bessel A. *The Body Keeps the Score: Brain, Mind, and Body in the Healing of Trauma.* New York: Viking, 2014.

Von Franz, Marie-Louise. *Psychotherapy.* Boston, MA: Shambhala, 1990.

Walker, Matthew P. *Why We Sleep: Unlocking the Power of Sleep and Dreams.* New York: Scribner, 2017.

Winnicott, Donald W. *Playing and Reality.* London: Routledge, 2010.

World Health Organization Social Change and Mental Health Violence and Injury Prevention. "Report of the Consultation on Child Abuse Prevention." Geneva, Switzerland: World Health Organization, 1999. Accessed November 23, 2020. https://apps.who.int/iris/handle/10665/65900.

Zoja, Eva Pattis. *Where Soul Meets Matter: Clinical and Social Applications of Jungian Sandplay Therapy.* Asheville, NC: Chiron, 2018.

INDEX

A

Abuse, sexual. *See* Sexual abuse
Active suicidal thoughts, 22-23. *See also* Suicide
Adult (legal age of majority), 4
Aizenstat, Dr. Stephen, 86
Alcohol use/abuse, 5, 37
Ambivalent Goddesses blog (Kerr), *x*
American Psychological Association, 3–4
Anger
    "Big T" Trauma and, 79
    imaginal dialogues and, 70–71
    impact of sexual abuse and, 5, 36
    posttraumatic stress disorder (PTSD) and, 79
Anniversaries of trauma, 96–97
Anxiety
    impact of sexual abuse and, 4, 36
    leaning in technique and, 52
    triggers and flashbacks and, 82
Art therapy, 64
Assessments, 26
Authentic healing, *xii*, 47, 99, 101

B

Bad days, 98-99
Belly Breaths exercise. *See* Seven Belly Breaths exercise
Big Skills, 63–65
"Big T" Trauma, 77–80
Binge eating, as symptom, 36
Blame. *See also* Self-blame
    "Big T" Trauma and, 78
    making sense of sexual abuse and, 12
    other people's reactions to sexual abuse and, 12–15
    talking with others and, 15
Bodily sensations
    Body Check exercise and, 59–62
    getting Too Cold and, 43
    getting Too Hot and, 39
    identifying when things are Just Right, 45–46
    impact of sexual abuse and, 37
    making sense of sexual abuse and, 13–14
    memories and, 10–11

Donate

Go to www.FirstHaven.org to make a donation or request additional copies. When you donate, you may also specify where to send copies.

First Haven is a 501(c)(3) nonprofit organization providing timely psychological self-help information to people ages 15 and up who have experienced sexual abuse. Our flagship guide, *Tending the Wound Sexual Abuse: An Introduction*, is distributed at no cost to crisis centers, agencies, and organizations directly serving those in need. First Haven's Federal Tax ID (EIN) is 85-1004178.

To donate by mail, make checks payable to First Haven. Mail to:

> First Haven
> 901 Paverstone Drive, Suite 9
> Raleigh NC 27615

Donate or request additional copies at:

www.FirstHaven.org